Praise for *Principal in Balance*

"In *Principal In Balance*, Jessica Cabeen embraces her vulnerability to illuminate the challenges and feelings many leaders face. Filled with research, personal stories, anecdotes, gentle reminders, and practical ideas from her years of experience as a school leader, she provides you with a pathway back to living the work-home life you want to lead."

— **Jimmy Casas**,
Leadership Coach, Educator, Author, Speaker

"Jessica provokes you to self-reflect on leading without margin, while she graciously gifts you with her own transparency of her glows and grows of self-caring while in leadership. Her chapters embark you on a journey that has allowed us to revisit our own priorities as individuals, parents, and most importantly, as life partners."

— **Dr. Kevin and Mrs. Crystal Armstrong**

"In *Principal in Balance*, Jessica Cabeen was able to put into words the honest journey of these past few years of the principalship. Jessica's vulnerable accounts of leadership, both at school and at home, helped me to name some of the same emotions that I have experienced. Her actionable, solution-driven strategies provide the next steps to sustainability. This will be a book that I will always keep close to reference and share readily with other leaders."

— **Beth Houf**,
Proud Principal, Fulton Middle School,
NASSP 2022 National Principal of the Year

"*Principal in Balance* is an urgent call to action for all Pre-K-12 educators and professionals to disrupt the chaos of 'busyness' in leadership to reconnect, recenter, rekindle, and rejuvenate our souls and humanity. Principal Cabeen provides practical wisdom essential to reclaim our dignity, exhausting opportunities without losing ourselves, and model self-love, self-knowledge, and self-actualization."

— **Dau Jok, Ph.D.**,
Executive Director of Diversity, Equity, and Inclusion,
West Des Moines Community Schools, West Des Moines,
IA | CPT in the United States Army Reserve

"Jessica Cabeen not only brings solid research-based counsel, but speaks out of a transparent, authentic heart formed through significant hardship. I so appreciated her honesty and grace."

— **David Schmus**,
Executive Director, Christian Educators

"Jessica Cabeen is an authentic leader who uses her personal story of triumph, success, failures, and setbacks to help other leaders reflect and redefine their purpose. *Principal in Balance* is full of leadership strategies that are focused on helping leaders become better versions of themselves."

— **Sanée Bell, Ed.D.**,
District Leader, Author, and Speaker

"My 35-year journey as a K-8 teacher and principal has been an amazing experience, but also a very challenging one. I prayed one day I would find the handbook to help me thrive and survive as a leader and a father, and I found it in *Principal in Balance*. Jessica Cabeen had me thinking so much throughout the book about finding a much needed balance, but also being more forgiving and kind to myself. If you read this book and don't feel like you can live a life worth leading and living, then you need to read it again. I am ready to lead and change education for another 10 years. Thanks Jess!"

— **Salome Thomas-EL, Ed.D**
(AKA Principal EL), Award-winning teacher, principal and author

"While each of us is a work in progress, it's rare to come across an author who is so transparent about it, while evolving with the turn of every page. Cabeen has given us a charge, in the form of a book that will educate you, challenge you, provoke you, and speak to you. What impressed me most about *Principal in Balance* is how she embraces what Jim Collins called 'the genius of and' vs. 'the tyranny of or.' She doesn't offer the false dichotomy of a principal being effective as a leader 'or' living a balanced life. She offers relatable advice, relevant research, and practical tools to move school leaders down the path of being both effective at work and whole at home. Within two chapters, I found myself setting intentions to be a better version of myself."

— **Kenneth Williams**,
nationally recognized trainer, speaker,
coach and consultant in leadership and school culture

Principal in Balance

Leading at Work and
Living a Life

Jessica M. Cabeen

JB JOSSEY-BASS™
A Wiley Brand

Library of Congress Cataloging-in-Publication Data:

Names: Cabeen, Jessica, author.
Title: Principal in balance : leading at work and living a life / Jessica
  M. Cabeen.
Description: First Edition. | San Francisco : Jossey-Bass, [2023] |
  Includes bibliographical references and index.
Identifiers: LCCN 2022060368 (print) | LCCN 2022060369 (ebook) | ISBN
  9781119885764 (Paperback) | ISBN 9781119885771 (Adobe pdf) | ISBN
  9781119885788 (epub)
Subjects: LCSH: School principals—Handbooks, manuals, etc. | Educational
  leadership. | Goal (Psychology) | Time management. | Self-management
  (Psychology) | Boundaries—Psychological aspects. | Mindfulness
  (Psychology)
Classification: LCC LB2831.9 .C33 2023 (print) | LCC LB2831.9 (ebook) |
  DDC 371.2/012—dc23/eng/20230103
LC record available at https://lccn.loc.gov/2022060368
LC ebook record available at https://lccn.loc.gov/2022060369

Cover Design: Wiley
Cover Image: © Jack_the_sparow/Shutterstock
SKY10043066_022123

Let the words of my mouth and the meditation of my heart be acceptable in your sight, O Lord, my rock and my redeemer. Psalm 19:14

Contents

Foreword

I accepted my first principal job 17 years ago. It meant a move across the state of Wisconsin to a place our family had never been. My wife and two sons, ages five and two at the time, packed up the truck and started what we were convinced was going to be the best adventure ever. In October of that first year, I remember walking into my house after a particularly difficult Thursday at school. Student issues, staff issues, parent issues, and supervisor issues all seemed to hit on a crisp, cool, Wisconsin fall day. I saw the boys and my wife at the kitchen table getting ready to eat dinner as I fumbled into the house exhausted and put my bag down. I sat down at the table, famished from not eating anything while at school, and began to attack the wonderful meal my wife prepared for everyone. After what seemed to be only a few minutes I looked up from my plate and the boys were gone. My extremely supportive wife was looking my way and I asked her where the boys had gone. Her response was "Your son just asked you three questions about your day and you never even picked your head up. We need to figure this thing out, really quickly."

I would love to tell you that from that moment I have been an incredible husband and a wonderful father who has everything figured out, but that's simply not true. I absolutely have struggled and that comes with the job. Having said that, when we go and go and go and do and do and do, we don't take a step back to realize the impact of go, go, go and do, do, do, both positively and negatively. Often, we look back and can't remember how we got there. That is not balance, and we simply can't attain our best selves when we live a life without it.

Leadership is hard, and what often happens is the people who we go home to, who love us the most and give us the most latitude, often get the least of us because of what is happening at school. We go home and think about other people's kids and families while we try to engage with our own. Conversely, if we haven't found balance at home, we spend the day leading a group of hundreds or thousands while thinking about what we are missing at home. Either way, success is limited in both areas.

Jessica Cabeen has found a way to articulate the struggles of balance while finding meaningful ways to adjust practice and help you succeed both at school and at home. The quotes are inspirational and provide hope, but the practical application of what you can do as a leader, to not only move forward but feel better, is what kept the pages turning for me. There are so many resources out there that provide inspiration with no plan, and though all are engaging in the moment, few have found a way to help me move forward as a leader, both at school and at home.

Principal in Balance elicits hope, but then gives you something you can do to turn the hope into success for you and those you lead. The ground rules did just that . . . they grounded the work in the why. The gentle reminders made me laugh, but also think about things I have put on autopilot. Doing the homework put the thoughts into action in a way that wasn't overwhelming and yet I could see little wins in the action taking place every day.

You are going to love *Principal in Balance*. You are going to come back to it. You are going to reference it with those you lead. I only wish it was sitting on that kitchen table 17 years ago.

– Joe Sanfelippo, PhD
2019 ED DIVE National Superintendent
of the Year, author, and speaker

About the Author

 **Jessica** is the Principal of Alternative Educations Programs in Austin, Minnesota. Previously, she was the principal of Ellis Middle School in Austin, Minnesota, and the principal of the "Happiest Place in Southeastern Minnesota," the Woodson Kindergarten Center. She has been an assistant middle school principal, a special education assistant director, and special education teacher.

Jessica was named the 2021 ED DIVE National Principal of the year, 2017 Minnesota National Distinguished Principal of the Year, and was awarded the NAESP/VINCI Digital Leader of Early Learning Award in 2016. She is a NAESP Middle Level Fellow and a Future Ready Principal. Jessica is the author of *Hacking Early Learning* and co-author of *Balance Like a Pirate, Unconventional Leadership*, and *Lead with Grace: Leaning into the Soft Skills of Leadership*.

She is a sought-after speaker and trainer and enjoys getting to learn and lead with other educators across the nation. Jessica enjoys connecting and growing her Professional Learning Network (PLN) on the socials. She can be found on Instagram, Facebook, and Twitter @JessicaCabeen.

But by far her favorite space is the one that involves being with her husband, Rob, sons Kenny and Isaiah, and, of course, the family dog, Herman.

Acknowledgments

A work in progress. That would be a great way to summarize the years of work that have gone into the publication of this book. This idea of becoming a principal in balance has been on my mind since 2016, and only has become a reality because of the support and encouragement of a very special team.

Ashante Thomas, thanks for supporting this work from the original pitch to final production. I am grateful for our partnership and your advice, support, and encouragement.

Sunnye Collins. If our edit communication was a Snapchat streak, we would be at an epic level. Thanks for your patience in helping me craft the words to make these stories come to life.

Pete Gaughan, Mary Beth Rosswurm, Julie Kerr, and the rest of the incredible team at Jossey-Bass: thanks for taking a chance and a stance on supporting the mental health of school administrators. Your belief in this project was humbling and inspiring.

I wouldn't be practicing what I speak to in the upcoming chapters if I didn't take time to thank those on the personal side of the principalship who helped to make this book happen.

To my husband, Rob. Twenty years of marriage, an incredible family, and an amazing journey we could have never expected in October of 2002 in Mason City, Iowa. Thank you for being my best friend and biggest cheerleader through everything.

Kenny—little did you know that you were the original reason for this shift of leading at work and living a life. Thank you for always reminding me about the importance of being your parent before your principal.

Isaiah—without you I wouldn't be here. You and I have been going to school together since kindergarten and I will be in the front row celebrating all your success moving forward. I have loved every moment of being your mom at home and your principal through many of your school years.

Manny. I never expected you to enter my story, but now I can't imagine life without you. You are an incredible young man who has impacted my life and leadership more than you know.

And finally—to the staff at Ellis Middle School. Very few administrators could say their best years were the past five years (2017–2022), but I can. Thank you for your unwavering commitment to the seventh and eighth grade scholars in Austin, Minnesota. You have taught me over and over the importance of a school culture that values the person over the position, and what amazing things can occur when your school becomes part of your family.

PART I

THE GROUND RULES
OF BALANCE

When you live well, you lead well.

#PrincipalinBalance

The inspiration for this book came from an unexpected Friday in May. If you are an educator, you know nothing is expected, and there are always surprises in May, especially in May of 2021. On this Friday, I spent the morning dancing with my mask on and waving to 400 hybrid students in Ellis Middle School. I went into a six-hour planning session for the upcoming master schedule while trying to balance the 80 emails I received. I ran home quickly to let our pandemic puppy out at lunch, came back, crafted a few parent messages for our school messenger, and said goodbye to students as they got on buses for home and sports.

During the day, I was criticized, yelled at, and, at the end of the day, hung up on. At 4:00 p.m., my normal routine was to get my fifth coffee of the day and settle in for a few hours of work and emails while my teenagers were out and my husband was at work.

But not this Friday. On this day, I logged off and left school. I drove 40 minutes with no podcasts, music, emails, calls, or conferences—just quiet. I stood in Minnesota May weather (sleet/snow is always possible) and cheered on my eighth-grade son and his newly acquired sport: track. Typically, when I got home to get him off the bus from his meet, I would race home and finish up what came through when I was offline. Instead, this Friday, we drove to watch a friend's soccer game for another two hours. By the time I got home, I was so fulfilled from spending time with my son I didn't feel guilty about not putting in the usual 14-hour workday. So often as servant leaders we have a hard time learning when to stop and focus on ourselves. I just can't believe it took me a random Friday in May—well into my educational career—to realize it.

So, entering the later stages of my career, I have learned a lesson I wish I would have learned much earlier on: life is more than our title. Our primary priorities should rest outside of our day job.

I strive every day to be a better *Principal in Balance*. One who is learning to lead at work *and* have a life. One who embraces time in rest instead of resisting the chance to pause. A person who learns to let the angry phone calls go and lean into the relationships of those closest to me at school, and at home.

I am becoming a principal who recognizes I can't be good for anyone if I am not good to myself first. One who has embraced a regular morning routine that always involves some form of self-care. A principal who has broken up with her cell phone and continues to find ways to regulate tech to be productive, focused, and less distracted by beeps, tweets, and notifications.

These life lessons have been learned over the past 10 years on many unexpected Fridays. I have lost time with family because I prioritized emails and evening school activities over bedtime with a toddler. I almost lost friends because I always was distracted by emails, texts, and phone calls instead of focusing on who was right in front of me. And for a period, I lost myself and who I was supposed to be when the adoption of our son was disrupted.

So, how are you?

Are you in a season where you question why you are teaching or leading? Are you struggling with prioritizing what needs to get done and what you can delegate or just let go? Have you canceled or forgotten to schedule your own medical, dental, and counseling appointments because you just don't have time? Yet will you cover a colleague's class so they can make their own appointments? Do you remember the last time you went to dinner with friends, family, or your spouse? What about the last time you sat and read a book . . . for fun?

Teachers, paraprofessionals, administrative assistants, central office staff . . . please don't let the title of this book deter you from reading! Being a *Principal in Balance* is more than a school title but an opportunity to lead your own work and life no matter what your business card says.

Becoming a *Principal in Balance* is not an endpoint, but a journey. Whether you are in a season of struggle or walking into a new position with pride and accomplishment, we can all use a few gentle reminders to reflect, recalibrate, and refocus. This book tackles some of the biggest struggles educators have in reaching points of rest. It also offers tips in setting habits to establish long-term and meaningful routines that focus on you and your family first.

As a student of resiliency, a resistor of burnout, and a recent believer of the importance of daily rest, I have learned a lot about what it can look like to be a *Principal in Balance* on a Tuesday when you are three teachers short, or when you get to work and find out you have a sick child at home. Through these experiences, we will walk through ways to establish habits for health and navigate the hiccups to the plans you put in place.

I will admit, this is kind of a bold move to write a book on balance when I am still trying to figure it out.

Yup, I haven't found the unicorn, the perfect fit, or the magic key to making my life work every day. What I do have is a passion to make a difference, and an understanding I can't operate at an unsustainable pace for long.

You see it every day on social media, news outlets, and other channels: we are tired.

You hear it from friends, coworkers, and trusted colleagues in work and life: I need to quit.

You feel it in the perceived pressures from TV, popular opinion, and Facebook posts: if you aren't on all the time, you aren't living the life you should lead.

I have days where I am pulled back into the position of busyness as a badge of honor. I still struggle with understanding that sometimes I have to slow down to see exactly the direction I am trying to go. When you are used to going at an unsustainable pace, creating a normal rhythm seems selfish and slow. Finding joy in seeing margin in your calendar seems counterintuitive to the pace of filling every day in your planner and accounting for every minute in the day. And my heart still hurts when I say no to others because I need to stop and say yes to myself. When we are called to a career that prioritizes serving, it can create, unintentionally, a sense of sacrifice over ourselves, no matter what the cost.

In this work, I have learned a lot of lessons, and through this journey, I have been acknowledged in many ways.

In 2016, I received the NAESP/VINCI Digital Leader of Early Learning Award.

> ... I also struggled with feeling like I wasn't enough for the students
> I served and my family at home.

In 2017, I was awarded the National Distinguished Principal Award for the State of Minnesota.

> ... and in 2018 I was slammed on social media by fake accounts
> and false stories about my ability to lead in schools.

In 2019, I was speaking regularly and had published my fourth book.

. . . and in 2020 COVID was the lowest low of my career.

In 2021, I was recognized as the K-12 DIVE Education Awards Principal of the Year.

. . . and in the winter of 2022, I experienced daily anxiety attacks that at times incapacitated me at work and in life.

I don't share this with you for sympathy. I offer these examples (and trust me, I have many more) to highlight that this work will have ups and downs, and finding the balance requires you to find ways to stabilize the time between the highs and lows so the climb (and the fall) is not so hard when they happen.

SEEKING PLATEAUS IN THE PROCESS

There is an old saying: "The higher you climb, the harder you fall." I can take that to mean that the further you grow in your career, the more advanced you become and the accolades you achieve in your life, the harder it will hurt when someone or something tries to take it away, or you struggle in your daily walk of this work.

What I would challenge you to do with this work, and within this book, is to find the plateaus between the mountains and the valleys.

Recently, I went on a college visit with my son Kenny to my alma mater: the University of Wisconsin Eau Claire. It has incredible programs, great sports teams, a wonderful music program, and a killer hill on campus. It's not an exaggeration to say it is the largest Midwest mountain around. That hill was part of the reason I gladly moved off campus my junior year; the thing was straight up—both ways. So, when the tour started, I knew we were going to have to climb that hill. Mind you, I hiked that thing in my late teens and now 20-some years later I was going to tackle it again? My mind was gearing up for how hard it was going to be and how I could save face when my heart rate was racing. But while I was worried about what would go wrong, something happened. We stopped halfway.

In all my years of hiking and pushing through just to get to the top, I missed the plateau halfway up! The five minutes we spent catching our breath made up for the exhaustion I would have felt had we just kept going. By stopping, I also had a chance to slow down and look around. In climbing any mountain, there are always incredible views, but you miss it if your only focus is to finish.

Seeking balance will require you to use plateaus in the journey more than you think you should.

Try to use a plateau for a pause instead of pushing up a mountain that, when you reach the top, you realize you didn't want to climb.

Use a plateau to break your fall halfway when you realize you have taken on too much at work or in life and need to rest and recalibrate before you climb again.

Use a plateau to lean into when others' thoughts and opinions are keeping you in the weeds that slow down your abilities to lead at work and have a life.

And who knows? When you rest midway up (or recover from sliding down), you might see some incredible views and gain an important perspective on the life you want to live.

Ready to find the plateau and start the journey?

This book walks through the stages of establishing balance, boundaries, and ways to prevent burnout. Strategies for further work will also be included so you can find the one most applicable, whatever season you are in. We walk through this book in four stages, which are the guiding ground rules of the work.

Ground Rules of Balance. This section gives a detailed rationale for why we need to take care of ourselves, before we get into the work of caring for others. Through the lens of a practitioner enhanced with research and suggestions from professionals in the work of well-being, resiliency, and rest, this section has you set a foundation for the work ahead.

Dream Big. This section is all about setting and achieving goals while creating realistic plans for your passions. Before we can get into the how and what, it is important we create our why. Why do you want to lose weight? Why do you want a new position? Why do you feel called to pause on your professional life to work on starting a family, or form deeper relationships with the family you already have? Creating a why will help you throughout the book when things get hard (and they will).

Live Colorfully. This section explores how to thrive, not just survive. How in the world do you accomplish this in a day when hustle is many of our nicknames? Living Colorfully will require you to lead a different type of life. One that might go outside the traditional lines and be filled with color, not just shades of gray. In this segment, we will learn the importance of setting boundaries. Not just boundaries with people, but with our time, what gets stuck in our mind, and how technology can help, or hurt, this work.

Lead Boldly. This section puts you in the driver's seat of your learning. We review action plans and find ways to manage the hiccups before they become insurmountable hurdles. Feel confident in taking charge of your learning and learn how to cultivate habits to help you along the way.

Within each section, we set *Ground Rules* for the work you will engage in. Some of these rules are common sense, others will feel uncomfortable. I challenge you to lean into the discomfort and press forward in the chapter. Chances are, the aspects of balance that are the most uncomfortable will be the ones that push you to do something you never thought possible, or something you never thought you deserved.

This is hard work, no way around it. *Gentle Reminders* are just that. Things to consider as you practice the tenants of becoming a *Principal in Balance*. This is an opportunity to give yourself grace as you start to prioritize yourself and your health before anything else.

And just like anything else school-related, each chapter will have a section entitled *Doing the Homework*. The assignment will either help you make plans, create habits, or hold yourself accountable for the work in this book. Please don't forget to do this work! It is essential in becoming a *Principal in Balance* to put into practice what you are reading, gain perspective of how this work will flow, and prioritize daily self-care, soul-care, and resilience practices.

My hope for each of you is to have that unexpected Friday and free yourself from the burdens of others' expectations and plans and walk forward confident in your own skin and calling.

Let's disrupt what we think we should be doing and reconstruct life in better balance—one worth leading and living.

CHAPTER 1

Rationale for Resiliency

From the lowest pit to the top of the mountain,
How do you *thrive?*

#PrincipalinBalance

Every day I see students who demonstrate resilience from change, adversity, or trauma. My own son, who saw more in his first five years than most would in their entire life, continues to amaze and inspire me with his willingness to move forward no matter the setback. So why is it we can see resiliency and success in our own students, but not recognize the need for them in ourselves?

Do they need support, help, and a network to support practices to build resiliency at their unique leadership level? Absolutely. Do leaders struggle to see through the clouds and find the silver lining when work and life collide or collapse? Of course. Do leaders recognize the signs of burnout and seek help? Not always. Will they support and serve others through difficult experiences often at their own expense? A lot of the time.

That being said, let's take a tough look at what it takes to become more resilient in the face of changes, challenges, or chaos at work or home.

What is resiliency?

re · sil · ien · cy | \ ri-ˈzil-yən(t)-sē: an ability to recover from or adjust easily to adversity or change

Getting back up after a fall, looking for the silver lining, seeing the glass half full, bouncing back. You have heard them all, and sometimes while rolling your eyes. Whatever the saying, the meaning is consistent: resilience is the ability and flexibility to accept challenges. This requires a foundational purpose for why you have been called to this opportunity. Along with that, you need the skills to recover from any fall or falter that happens in the work.

There is another way to look at this. In non-academic terms:

Adjust *your nucleus*
so you don't *go nuclear.*

#PrincipalinBalance

Our nucleus is our core, beliefs, passions, and abilities to navigate life. When intact and stable, it gives us the ability to navigate the obstacles in front of us. We can often handle hiccups and detours in the path seamlessly. People might notice how calm you are amidst the chaos. Like the formal definition, my middle school girl example requires the same: grounded in purpose, willing to accept changes, and flexible with the results and the timing of the outcome.

However, when our nucleus is constantly attacked, it can start to crack, and things can leak out—causing a memorable nuclear moment. These moments can be different for everyone depending on the circumstance. It might mean blowing up at someone for a minor question. It could be crying over something that any other day wouldn't mean much of anything.

Nuclear to me is reminiscent of the "Help Me Help You" scene in the movie *Jerry Maguire*. Jerry was giving Rod Tidwell a little advice in regard to improving his off-the-field performance, and he refused the advice. Jerry suddenly goes into a full-on, three-year-old temper tantrum meltdown. His thought bubble pops, and he says everything he was thinking and ultimately causes Rod to laugh and end the scene with "You, my friend, are hanging on by a very thin thread."

Sound familiar? We have all had that nuclear moment. The difference between nuclear and not depends on the resiliency of your nucleus.

During the process of adopting a child, I read all the books and blogs, took the classes, and networked with other moms in various stages of the process. I attended the weekend bootcamps in which counselors, social workers, and adult adopted children prepared us for the worst by giving us strategies for the best. But in all those hours and all that research, I missed the chapter on what to do when your adoption is terminated. My therapist called it *ambiguous loss*. Which means loss without closure. A death without a body, an adoption without a child.

And that was the start of my long *Jerry Maguire* season.

During the weeks after the termination of our adoption, I experienced a wide range of emotions and struggled to find a rhythm as I returned to work the day after we were told the news. I would cry often and unexpectedly. I lost my appetite. I lost focus at work and home. The interactions that normally brought me joy felt like nothing. I was numb. In a way, I refused to come to terms with the situation. I continued to write in a journal for our son and planned to find a way to visit him later in life. I kept quiet about the loss to those who didn't know our story. Pretending it didn't happen was easier than feeling the emotions while retelling the story. Life felt different for a long time. And because I hadn't spent time developing resiliency, my nucleus was shattered. I had to find ways to build up a reserve for what was to come.

We have all overcome obstacles. Some of us have faced difficult traumas, and some of us demonstrate bravery in moving past a difficult situation or circumstance. When in it, we tend to overlook the importance of building up our resilience. This could include finding ways to manage emotions, redefining purpose, creating activities for stress relief, seeking self-care, and building self-regulation strategies.

Finally, with the help of a team of support at school and my spouse at home, I was able to find a therapist. This allowed me the opportunity to start working through the feelings of loss and find ways to rebuild the stamina of living life a little fuller after a loss.

During the months after the ambiguous loss, I found that rebuilding my self-care routine helped to create stability in my day. Finding a therapist to connect with allowed me to have someone look inside and help me to stop awfulizing and start finding purpose on this path I didn't intend to take. I regained my purpose of serving and supporting children and families as an assistant principal and started to find joy in my work.

After a few months of rebuilding this routine and reestablishing consistent resilience practices, something happened. This time it played out like a *Lifetime* movie: the adoption process was reinstated and a week later I was on a plane by myself traveling across the country to bring home a four-and-a-half-year-old boy. Through the struggles of the previous months, I was so fortunate to have built up consistent resiliency strategies that would help me prepare for the trips, falls, and failures to come.

BUILDING RESILIENCY

It doesn't take a significant event to put your resilience in check. And for all of us, March 2020 was the start of a long road ahead and a priority to build new protective factors to face the pivots, pressures, and pain to come.

During the spring of 2020, any resiliency reserves I had were spent. I thought if I just kept trying what had always worked, it would eventually click. I was wrong. Living through a pandemic while trying to lead a school from your basement and support your own children upstairs was a nonstop, chaotic series of events that only seemed to get worse. By May, I realized my pace, combined with my attitude, was not sustainable. Burnout, blow-ups, and breakdowns were occurring more often and I was slowly becoming someone I didn't recognize.

Realizing this was not going to go away in August, after the summer break, I decided to dig deeper into the research around resilience for myself, as well as for the educators and families I would serve again after the summer. A dear friend connected me with the work of Dr. Clay Cook, and by the end of June I started a course he offered online entitled *Becoming a Resilient Person: The Science of Stress Management and Promoting Wellbeing*. Through this course, I gained a deeper understanding of not only the importance of resilience in my personal life, but how to support other educators in building their own reserves as we returned to school amidst a pandemic. One of the key aspects of the course I continue to live by is that a resilient person is someone who:

- Purposely strives to be as mentally and psychically healthy as possible.
- Possesses the confidence to effectively cope with and manage stressful situations.
- Is compassionate toward self and others.
- Demonstrates grit or perseverance even in the face of adversity.
- Focuses on the positive and fulfilling aspects of life. (*Becoming a Resilient Person | ECFS311x* 2015)

Armed with this knowledge, and weeks of depth of understanding of this work, I returned to leading a school amidst a pandemic with ideas for application to help support a more resilient school culture by trying to live and lead it myself. Some of the basic applications of these practices included:

- Setting boundaries between school and work, by blocking off my calendar at night and taking email off my cell phone.
- Keeping up with my daily morning routines and not starting to work until I physically arrived at work (or entered my basement office during distance learning).
- Continuing to offer Positive Office Referrals to both staff and students and regularly asking staff to recommend other staff for shout-outs in our monthly staff memo.

- Becoming more vulnerable with those I worked with about the struggles I was experiencing and in turn building a deeper trust and a positive school culture that embraced challenges and prioritized purpose over perfection.
- Re-establishing a practice of identifying three good things that happened the day before and three things I was looking forward to in order to reframe situations and build daily gratitude.

Looking back, many of the things I started doing didn't take a ton of time, just intentional effort. However, by building up my reserve of resilient practices, the falls don't hurt as much and I am able to get back up quicker and start moving forward again. The foundation of becoming a *Principal in Balance* is building up a set of activities, coping strategies, and supports that will become your playlist of resiliency reserves.

These things are either done regularly for overall well-being or actions you take when you are in a dark season. In the Live Colorfully section of the book, we look at these reserves through the lens of self-care and soul-care, and by the end of the book you will have developed a list of activities that are authentically yours. You can draw from them when needed and include them in your everyday life for balance maintenance.

RECOVERY EFFORTS

Being resilient means you have built up the strength to navigate difficult situations. It is the ability to remain calm when things are falling apart all around you. Learning adaptive strategies allows you to engage that ability to thrive (not simply survive) through challenging circumstances. In the next few chapters, we address stress and emotional regulation, but in this chapter we lean into the importance of self-regulation for school leaders and educators.

In your work as educators, the aspect of self-regulation for students is fairly common practice. The ability to self-regulate behavior is one of the most important protective factors in relation to resilience and should be fostered especially in at-risk youth (Artuch-Garde et al. 2017, p. 8). We spend a great deal of time reading and researching strategies to support all students in dealing with the process of self-regulation during stressors. So, with all this understanding of the impact of proactive resilience practices, why do we stop short of dedicating time developing strategies for self-regulation for the adults in our school?

Self-regulation is essential in leadership development. Think about it: it isn't about what you say, but how you say it. Leadership is challenging in any career. Leading in a school with multifaceted challenges, stakeholders, and in a service-orientated field can require a depth of resiliency that other careers may not need. If you are not self-regulated when you enter a stressful situation, your response might be too strong, too soft, or not taken in the correct context, not because of what you said but the body language, tone, or demeanor in which you said it.

Understanding this early on as the foundation for becoming a *Principal in Balance* is important. Focusing on resilience and self-regulation will afford you a deeper understanding of the need to push forward and past the practices we have been doing, and doing, and doing with mixed results.

On a regular basis, I can enter a hard conversation that impacts all participants on a deeply emotional level. I can be the "hero" in the conversation, the one who has the right answers, the funding, the resources, or the positional power to make things happen. But I can also be the "villain," the one who delivers difficult news, the one who is pitted between teacher and student in a no-win situation.

I have titled myself as the ultimate fun-sucker on campus. The one who has to say no when everyone wants me to say yes. The one who has to think about rules, regulations, and safety implications when others just want to have fun. Being regulated in every interaction is essential because any other response than one that is calm and clearly communicated just doesn't work. Being a school leader is multifaceted. Being the one who is stable on rough seas is just one characteristic needed to do this work well.

You can't be *self-regulated* unless you are grounded in *resiliency*.

#PrincipalinBalance

It is never about what you say, but how you say it and how you receive feedback from others. As a middle school assistant principal, I felt like my office was a port-a-potty. People would come in and unload on me. Teachers were frustrated with student behavior. Students were disappointed in teacher interactions. Parents were angry with a process or plan. Community members let loose because of traffic patterns at the start and end of the day. People would come in on a regular basis, unload, and leave feeling "better." I would like to think that somehow my energy, my response, or my feedback helped to smooth over a circumstance or make the other person feel better about a situation. I really do enjoy listening and helping others, but I just have to be cautious not to take on all of their problems.

Back to the port-a-potty office. When I am well-regulated, I can handle others' complaints and frustrations. I can lean into reframing, self-control, compassion, and gratitude. But if I don't get enough sleep the night before, the smallest piece of feedback can feel insurmountable. I can internalize and awfulize others' problems. It is like the port-a-potty is out of hand sanitizer and it needs to be closed for cleaning.

HOW DO YOU GET BACK UP AFTER YOU FALL DOWN?

We have to start being okay with saying I am not okay. There will be times in your day when you just need a minute, to prepare yourself, to regulate, or to pause before you respond. As we work through this book you will learn many strategies. However, it is important to remember that we are not going to be perfect in pursuing a more balanced life, but we need to start taking time for ourselves intentionally and building resiliency to help us succeed in work and life.

You need to make time to slow down and really sit in and identify your feelings before moving forward. By focusing inward on identifying how you are really feeling, you can find appropriate strategies to self-regulate and be ready to respond to others in calm and predictable ways.

You may be saying to yourself, "Okay, Cabeen. I get why self-regulation and managing stress is essential in leadership development, but how do I do it? And more importantly, when do I find the time?" I have found it is essential to be grounded in why something is important before you get to how it works and what happens when it is implemented.

How many times in a stressful day or season do you quickly respond to the "how are you" question with "fine"? And how many of us use the response "fine" as fast pass around identifying how we are really feeling? Too often we assume speaking out about our real feelings makes us weaker leaders. But more often, those we lead will follow leaders who lean into vulnerability and authenticity, not perfection and pushing down how they feel.

As Daniel Goleman states in his best-seller *Emotional Intelligence*, "If your emotional abilities aren't in hand, if you don't have self-awareness, if you are not able to manage your distressing emotions, if you can't have empathy and have effective relationships, then no matter how smart you are, you are not going to get very far" (Goleman 2006). So often we only focus on the development of site plans, staff meeting agendas, interview questions, and the tactical aspects of leading. When there is a high focus on that and no focus on the emotional side of leading, we lose the opportunity to leverage the higher impact of integrating our authentic selves into how we lead, not just from how we have watched others.

Within my consulting and coaching work, I see too often two different interpretations of the same situation. Leaders see themselves as having strong communication skills, high buy-in with their staff, and favorable feedback from those they serve. When I speak with staff, they say the opposite. They are afraid of what leader they will get that day, the bite and the bark of the message hurts, and way too often the unrealistic fear of retaliation for speaking up about ways to improve tends to silence great people or force them to leave. Regardless, it is awful on all ends and if it continues, it will leave us with schools with unhappy staff, stressed-out students, and leaders who are not clued in to how the minor physical and emotional responses have impacted the school culture in major ways.

TAKE THE TIME TO CALM YOUR CORE

Another way to look at your nucleus is to look at everything everyone can't see. As an educator, you may have come across Sylvia Duckworth's Iceberg Illusion visual (Eichenlaub 2018). This visual shows that people tend to only see the visible part of the iceberg (success), but not all the things below the surface that are required to achieve that success.

As principals, so much of our work mirrors this visual and the mindsets we need to be successful. Below the surface is the deep and sometimes dark work that is not seen by others. This might include:

- Daily check-ins with struggling students.
- The supportive texts, emails, calls, and cards to staff.

- Late nights and early mornings to finish the tasks that didn't get done due to sub shortages, student meltdowns, or other unpredicted events in the day.
- Hours, weeks, and months spent planning how the schedule will be built, monitoring the success of the new site plan, or reviewing the implementation cycle of the new curriculum adoption.

And while at times this work can seem overwhelming and underappreciated, it is important to link the work beneath the surface to the success you are achieving at the tip of the iceberg.

Resiliency Is the Willingness to Work Towards Becoming Balanced

So, while not everyone may fully understand all that goes on beneath the surface to accomplish the outcomes people see, please take time to celebrate the success at the tip of the iceberg, big and small. You deserve it.

Throughout this chapter, we learned what it is to be resilient, why it is important, and what it looks like when we are leaning into it or when we are fighting it. Without resilience, you will lose your balance. Resilience keeps you grounded, focused, and healthy so you are ready to tackle any obstacle.

GENTLE REMINDER: CONFIDENCE WITH YOUR COMPETENCE

Falling down is hard, but when you are confident in your competence in the work you are doing it will give you the strength to get back up.

Doing the Homework: Calming Your Core

Identify three activities that help you strengthen your core and give you preventive measures to maintain your nucleus before going nuclear. I have included a few sample situations to help guide your process.

How do you regulate after a negative conflict or conversation with a parent, coworker, or employee?

What works for you to calm your core after a stressful day at work? How can you pause and put away the stress of the day before you walk in the door at home? In other words, how do you reset to avoid walking in the door and lashing out?

A project or a plan you put together for a student activity or your site plan just broke down. How do you regulate your emotions before you respond?

CHAPTER 2

Surge Capacity, Stress, and Survival

What *has to go,*
in order for *you to grow?*

#PrincipalinBalance

The terrible, no-good, awful day. I sometimes call them bad hair days, spicy mocha days, or "What is up with you, Cabeen?" days, as a middle schooler might say. Sometimes these days start off fine, but as the day goes on, nothing goes your way. In any field, circumstance, or season of life, these days are unavoidable. However, how we respond to these days is within our control. Developing healthy responses to unexpected curve balls builds resilience and helps us handle stress in a much more balanced way.

Stress \ 'stres: to subject to physical or psychological stress

Stress is unavoidable. There are times when stress can be helpful, and other times stress can be harmful. This work starts with identifying stress, the good, the bad, and the ugly.

The Yerkes-Dodson law explains that stress can be good, bad, and necessary in all seasons. Some stress is necessary to get the ball rolling. A deadline, a project, managing two different sports seasons for two teenagers? That is stress. It motivates us to get things done; it gives a timeline, so we don't sit on it too long, and it rewards us for completing the tasks at hand.

But take that stress and add on covering multiple classrooms without subs, having to terminate or reprimand an employee, responding to a hostile parent or a teenager who posted something inappropriate on social media, and the stress goes through the roof. And all the balls you were juggling just drop to the ground.

When you are not stressed at all, your performance is impacted by a lack of motivation. When your stress is high, your performance is negatively impacted by anxiety and a flight-or-freeze response. When you have manageable stress, your performance is optimal.

Think about a time when you had low to no stress (I know, think hard). What did you catch yourself doing? Maybe bingeing on a Netflix series,

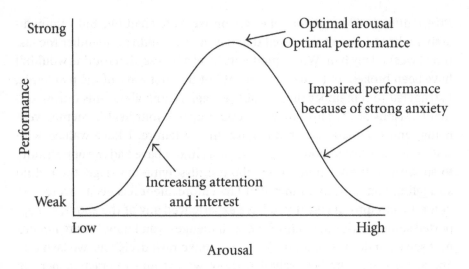

scrolling on your social media feeds, or surfing the internet with no real purpose. Breaks in the school year can cause me to not just unwind but become completely unproductive. Every year (and I am going on over two decades of applied experience here), I have a list of things I plan to do over the winter or summer break. Oh, I will organize the closets, I will prepare a meal plan schedule for the upcoming months, I will start learning a new language, I will get up and exercise every day on break, or I will go visit a few friends or spend time with family unplugged. Can I be honest? I was awful at fulfilling any of these tasks. The end of the break sneaks up on me and I race to try to accomplish at least one thing, but feel guilty about all the time lost because I had no motivation to do anything.

Now let's go to the other end of the pendulum. High (over-the-top) stress can cause almost the same reaction.

I remember when we first went into distance learning. There were so many decisions and so many unknowns. I remember finishing up meetings at the end of the long days and having no idea what I wanted for dinner. During the pandemic, I was on a weekly webinar for leaders developed by the National Association of Elementary School Principals (NAESP) called

Principaling in Place. Before one session we were chatting, and I immediately realized I hadn't showered that day, and I couldn't remember the last time I washed my hair. With a moderate level of stress, that routine wouldn't have been broken, but during the height of the first wave of the pandemic, I struggled to remember the day of the week. Think about this during difficult seasons of your life and how stress impacts your health, mental well-being, and occupational productivity. In my tenure, I have walked with staff who have lost a spouse, a parent, or a child. I have had the opportunity to sit with staff after finding out about a dissolving marriage, their child struggling mentally, and times that law enforcement has been involved in domestic circumstances. If you have experienced any of the above, or supported someone through one of these challenges, you know. We are not our best selves under this kind of stress. We make rash decisions, we lash out, and we are not our best selves in how we act and interact in person, and online.

So when situations, events, or circumstances seem out of control, how can we bring back order and calm to chaos? If you have stabilized stress before the event, the impact will feel different than if you were already spiraling out of control.

The curve visualizes what so many of us already knew—

It is important to *have stress,*
and to identify how to *stabilize life*
when stress is no longer optimal,
but out of control.

#PrincipalinBalance

Make sense? Sure. But how do you control the stress, especially when you are trying to juggle all those balls in the air? Before we get into the details, it is important to lay the foundation for support to help stabilize stress in all aspects of our daily lives.

So, let's talk about those curveballs. They can range from a minor hiccup in our day to a major detour in our professional or personal path. No matter what size or duration of the curve ball—our response matters.

UNDER PRESSURE

When I think about how I handle stress, the David Bowie/Queen song "Under Pressure" always comes into my mind. Specifically, these lyrics:

Pressure pushing down on me
Pressing down on you, no man ask for

(Queen Ft. David Bowie, "Under Pressure"
[Official Lyric Video] 2017)

Stress can feel like a physical pressure or visceral reaction to a situation in your life. Think about a time when you were stressed. Was your breathing labored? Did you feel your heart race? How about your physical demeanor? Hands clenched? Jaw tightening? Stress can show up in our bodies before our brains have time to slow down the effects if we don't have the right safety nets in place to prevent wear and tear on our bodies and minds.

Working with teens is an unending roller coaster. You can walk into a school day with hugs and high fives and leave with bruises (physical and emotional), and carry those back to your car in the parking lot. It was during my second year as the principal of the middle school that I had an experience in which my stress levels reached new, and unhealthy, heights. On a Sunday afternoon, my phone started to buzz nonstop. A student had posted of a possible school shooting for the following week, and within an hour a team was assembled and plans were in place to address the concern. And while the threat was found not to be credible, a few hours after it was reported, the wheels were already in motion with a plan for enhanced safety. Students, parents, and community stakeholders were on high alert. Our district team took extra precautions and later that night communication went out to families about the enhanced security for the upcoming week.

In education, so much happens and because this work is with our children, the details cannot be shared publicly. This is when social media starts to fill in the cracks. The incident quickly shifted from a poor choice by a teenager to bad parenting, bad teaching, and bad leading. The news vans showed up and parked outside our school looking for anyone to interview, all while posting comments and stories that fueled the fire we were trying to put out. If you want a course in humility, read the comments on those posts. People who thought our school was in another state started coming after us, our kids, and parents. If you have been on the receiving end of one of these threads, you get it. If you have ever participated in one of these threads, I would encourage you to breathe, think, and wait to comment or post. Do your best to fact check, or phone the people directly responsible, instead of posting a social media thread.

The next three weeks of my life were spent at work, 24/7. Even when I wasn't physically there my mind was at school. No sleep, no food, and no tears left. I was a wreck. I lost 10 pounds and utilized TV, wine, and Cheetos to numb the emotional pain of trying to protect the school, staff, and students I loved from something completely out of my control. Trying to fix something that wasn't your fault and then dealing with communication outside of your school is a practice of humility, clarity, and recalibrating boundaries.

STRESS REGULATION

Through that season and circumstance, I started back with a therapist and leaned into what I do well: reading and research. That's when I found Amit Sood, MD. My copy of his book is highlighted more colorfully than a fridge full of school pictures. You can't help but lean into what he says. Sood states the following in regard to the key ways to reduce stress in our lives: "I haven't found any stressor in my life or that of anyone I've met that couldn't be healed by using the five principles of gratitude, compassion, acceptance, higher meaning, and forgiveness" (Sood 2013, p. 91). So, let's break down how to practically apply these principles.

Gratitude

Building upon this with the foundation of resiliency requires a solid grasp of gratitude, reflection, and reframing to see growth through the weeds. In a stress response, instead of focusing on what went wrong, try to see what went right. In the situation above, while I couldn't prevent the student from making the choices they did, I could develop response systems to support families through situations out of our direct control. We put together information in regard to supporting their children's social media use at home, engaged in conversations around developmentally appropriate topics, and continued to positively engage with stakeholders. And throughout those challenging weeks, whatever was being posted, emailed, or left as hurtful voicemails, I continued to show up—greeting students as they walked into school, with my head held high.

Gratitude and the work of building this skill, at times, can be wrongly identified as toxic positivity. Those who continually choose to see the glass half full know the depleting factors involved; they just don't solely focus on them. Emily and Ameila Nagoski stress the following in their book: "Being grateful for good things doesn't erase the difficult things" (Nagoski and Nagoski 2020, p. 208).

During my miracle morning routine (more about this later), I write down three people I was grateful for the day before and why. During a school year, I have challenged myself to intentionally recognize every staff member in the building by sending a card home with a specific word of gratitude. I make a point of stopping and giving positive praise to students daily. While all of this can be seen to establish and maintain a healthy school culture, I see it as a way to maintain my sanity and see the good in any situation, even the really bad ones.

Compassion

Along with gratitude, compassion toward others can have a positive effect on our own resilience. By leaning into our empathetic side, we can gain a deeper understanding of others' trouble or trauma and support them moving through it. Often our stress comes from an assumption of ill intent from another or a perception that they are expecting more from us than we can provide. Compassion allows you to gain insight from another before assuming negative impact.

When my stress impacts my relationships with others, I try to practice the following: before I respond harshly or assume a negative impact from another, I think about three things this person positively contributes to the setting we are in (home, school, community). If I can't think of three, it is not the time to address whatever the issue might be.

There is one caution to address early on in this work.

Compassion fatigue is detrimental, so moderation is important. People working within a caring field, or those who care for others in the home or extended family have a higher likelihood of succumbing to the needs of others at our own expense. We will look at the importance of boundaries and bandwidth to prevent compassion fatigue later in the book.

Acceptance

Spoiler alert: it is not all about you. In the work of resilience it is rarely about you. Nor is it always your fault. Learning how to accept things and move past them is foundational in becoming more resilient in work and life. Things happen, mistakes are made, and sometimes things just occur that we have no explanation for. Knowing that is one thing but applying it when you are the victim of an act or decision can be challenging.

Moving past that social media incident in our school was essential in my ability to regulate stress and build my resilience for future situations. Because I moved past it, I developed ways to support my stress response for the next fight or social media meltdown. Without these supports, future events would have triggered the unresolved feelings, emotions, and physical responses from the first one. And each of these incidents would keep building and eventually burn me out. When we harbor hard feelings toward others it is difficult to be fully present, or really forgive and move forward.

Many times, in my career as a middle school assistant principal and principal, I have had students come back and tell me, "Wow, I was awful to you when I was in school." And you know what? I rarely remember that part of the person. I usually remember the positive interactions or times when things went well. Accepting that, just like ourselves, others are not perfect either is important in serving your purpose and supporting others, without looking back or dragging up history to move forward.

Acceptance doesn't mean agreement.

#PrincipalinBalance

Acceptance means an awareness and understanding of what has happened and learning how to move forward from it. By holding on to a circumstance or spinning on a situation, you lose the opportunity to accept, learn, and grow from it. In the moment, holding on and harboring sound easy, but in the long run, letting it go and moving forward is the faster track toward increasing your resilience for whatever is to come.

Higher Meaning

Finding a greater purpose in difficult seasons allows you to see past challenges and affords opportunities to see what positive things could come from this experience. Keeping things in perspective and reflecting on previous challenges also helps you see the higher purpose in what happened.

Try this activity. Think of a difficult situation you have gone through—a breakup, a change in job, a loss of someone in your life. Looking back, list three things you have learned because of that situation. Stepping back and looking at the bigger picture can give you a broader perspective and an opportunity to build skills you will use in the long term.

Forgiveness

Asking for forgiveness can be a challenge. In all honesty it can be really hard. So often we can find faults in others, without first seeing faults in ourselves.

This isn't a sign of weakness, but rather of vulnerability. This also helps us to lean into our mistakes, and then let . . . them . . . go. Holding on to mistakes and mishaps only hurts us in the long run. Asking for forgiveness and moving on helps us move forward with a better sense of what to do (or not to do) the next time.

STRESS, SURGE CAPACITY, AND SEEKING SOLACE

Tara Haelle first introduced me to the concept of surge capacity in her article "Your 'Surge Capacity' Is Depleted—It's Why You Feel Awful." She shares her experiences as a high-performing journalist who started slipping and struggling to juggle the balls of her career and support her children through the pandemic. Motivation was low, frustration was high, and there seemed to be no end in sight. In the article, she compares the pandemic with the term *ambiguous loss* and how the situation people were experiencing was a form of unresolved loss.

In school terms, teachers lost the opportunity to interact with students in person, every day, in a rhythm and routine they had experienced as a student. Major events and milestones were postponed or just canceled, and people moved forward in a fog waiting for the next thing to drop.

Tara's article gives a new perspective to the work and understanding of surge capacity and the implications on those of us trying to do it all, and getting nothing done.

Surge \ 'sərj: to rise suddenly to an excessive or abnormal value

ca · pac · i · ty|\kə-'pa-sə-tē: an individual's mental or physical ability

Tara quotes Dr. Ann Masten's work in her article to describe our own abilities to understand surge capacity: "Surge capacity is a collection of adaptive systems—mental and physical—that humans draw on for short-term survival in acutely stressful situations, such as natural disasters." The problem here is that many people today are constantly in a state of acutely stressful situations, with no end in sight. In the article, she shares similar coping strategies that support regulating surge capacity, stabilizing stress, and building up that resilience reservoir we need for the next time we gather the strength to get up after a fall. These included:

- **Acceptance.** We have to come to an understanding that things are not where we want them to be. By accepting, we can move forward and be flexible in the outcomes because we know that sitting in resistance and denial will just keep us stuck.
- **Adjust Expectations.** I have characterized this as 70% is your best right now. Getting through a traumatic event or thriving through surge capacity means you will not be perfect. The sooner you recognize that, the quicker you can move ahead.
- **Recognize signs of grief.** Stress, surge capacity, and resilience require you to acknowledge the hard parts so you can identify your feelings in the process and find strategies to support your emotional health.
- **Flexibility and fulfillment.** Being flexible through a stressful season, asking for help, and refilling your resilience reserve will help you move forward.

I wish I could say that was the only school threat I have ever received. And my heart hurts for administrators, teachers, staff, students, families, and communities that are impacted by these events. But for now, we can still expect traumatic events to occur in, and out of, schools, and educators and leaders will have to jump back in and respond, but with more tools to stabilize their surge capacity this time.

BURNOUT, BLOWUPS, AND BREAKDOWNS: WHEN YOUR SURGE CAPACITY IS SHOT

We are working toward building our resilience reserves, identifying good and bad stress, and working toward supportive practices during periods of surge capacity. But why? What happens if these things are not in place or sustainable during the peaks of the mountains of life, and the dark spots in the valleys?

burn · out | \ 'bərn-,au̇t: exhaustion of physical or emotional strength or motivation usually as a result of prolonged stress or frustration

Many teachers and principals are leaving the profession, or highly considering it.

But people—please stop using burnout as a catchall. Burnout is not a feeling. Burnout is not a medical condition. Burnout is a type of work-related stress. Burnout has often been used as an excuse to justify behavior. By naming someone else's condition as "burnout," you are justifying their behavior, or even worse, using it as an excuse for why you might not want to dig deeper to find out the feelings behind the behavior. In *Burnout: The Secret to Unlocking the Stress Cycle* (Nagoski and Nagoski 2020, p. xii), the authors found that the three components of burnout (emotional exhaustion, depersonalization, and decreased sense of accomplishment) are highly prevalent, especially in professions where people help people, like teachers.

Out of the three components, emotional exhaustion was most strongly linked to the negative impacts on our health, relationships, and work.

In social media, educators have gone from heroes to zeros in the eyes of a small pocket of the population, many of whom are not directly impacted by education themselves or their own children. These comments from the cheap seats can diminish the incredible work educators and leaders accomplish every day. I will blow off or diminish the compliment from someone I care about quicker than I sit with a piece of criticism from someone I don't know. How long do you sit with a piece of criticism versus a compliment?

Recently I was reading emails and received two of the kindest notes of affirmation from my favorite students. At the same time, I received a scathing voicemail from a family friend of a student I had been working with and recently had to suspend. The voicemail was hurtful and filled with assumptions of who I was and how I was trying to help. In that moment, the message took up more bandwidth and shook my confidence more than it should have. Instead of listening, I should have deleted and focused on the two emails from the students reminding me of my purpose and accomplishment. These feelings and situations can lead us down a road of burnout, blowups, and breakdowns.

But to be emotionally exhausted, you have to first feel an emotion, then ruminate and get stuck on it. Too often we sit in the feelings of others to the point that it takes over our own. As educators, we were never taught to put the oxygen mask on ourselves first. For some of us there is a deep sense of shame in taking time for ourselves to complete seemingly normal tasks like eating lunch, exercising, sleeping, and spending time with others we care about.

For me, getting stuck can look like worrying about how someone else is feeling or taking on much more of their burden than they even asked. I can ruminate on and replay situations over in my head well past the end of the day, sometimes even clouding my thinking at night when I am trying to sleep. The lack of sleep, boundaries, and prioritization of recognizing my own stress and emotional state lead right toward burnout. This can also spill into over-identifying feelings and behaviors of others. Be careful to over-identify others as having burnout when maybe they are just ruminating in space and need help finding a way out. And for once, ensure you are in a regulated space to help others before taking their burdens on top of your own.

SELF-CARE DURING STRESSFUL TIMES

Self-care is getting a bad rap. The social media warriors are on a warpath trivializing self-care as bubble baths, causing a sense of guilt or shame for those of us seeking it. Guilt for not making time to do it, shame for taking the time to care for yourself, and blaming others (like principals) for not giving it to you.

Here is the deal: self-care is not selfish. Hard stop.

Becoming a *Principal in Balance* is an explicit pass to prioritize self-care every day. An opportunity to take control of your priorities, set goals that are meaningful and achievable, and ultimately find a heightened quality of life at work and at home. So, let's look at self-care with a new lens and meaningful application to your own life.

Self-care is essential for stabilizing stress, minimizing surge capacity, and setting a course for a work-life balance that is sustainable and achievable.

- According to the Learning Policy Institute, "Nationally, the average tenure of a principal is about four years, and nearly one in five principals, approximately 18 percent, turn over annually. Often the schools that need the most capable principals, those serving students from low-income families, have even greater principal turnover."
- In NASSP's *Principal Leadership* magazine, it was found that "as many as 75 percent of principals experience stress-related symptoms that can affect their physical, emotional, and mental health."
- A 2021 Survey conducted by NASSP showed that "79% of principals report they have been working harder, 73% report working longer hours and 62% report having a harder time doing their job than ever before."

The work seems to be getting harder, and if we keep waiting for help from others, we will keep losing great people from this profession.

We need to change the conversations around self-care in education. *New York Times* columnist Tara Parker-Pope shares a new way to define self-care that might sustain past those who want to say it isn't needed: self-care ultimately is about setting priorities, setting boundaries, and finding purpose (Parker-Pope, 2021).

With this lens, self-care becomes an integrated part of your daily experience, not an extra. Not that scheduled hair appointment, but daily meditation. Stop thinking about spas and start thinking about enjoying healthy meals on a regular basis.

Key considerations for daily self-care integration include prioritizing you—all of you. And that starts with identifying your purpose. What are you called to do, and what unique gifts, talents, and attributes do you bring to the table? From there, how can your health and happiness work together to help you achieve your purpose on a regular basis?

This will end up becoming your North Star as you work through the chapters of this book. Coming back to your why will make your ways so much easier to navigate. Setting boundaries when you know what you are doing is so much easier to do and maintain. Priorities become crystal clear when the weeds of the daily demands and pressures from others are cleared away. This process is not easy, but it is worth it. I look back on my years navigating and recalibrating on this journey and don't regret for a second that I started it. I only wish I would have started years before 2016.

GENTLE REMINDER: PAUSE TO REFILL WHEN YOUR CAPACITY HAS OVERFILLED

There will be times in your work or life when your surge capacity is not only depleted but destroyed. At a time when your stress is off the charts, you will notice self-care goes right out the window with it. When (not if) that happens, use the following strategies to get yourself back on course.

What is going well right now at work? And in life? Identify three things in each area that are going well for you in work and in life.

Health	Happiness	Purpose

What are you going to continue to do to keep what is going well in work and life on your calendar and in your priorities?

Health	Happiness	Purpose

What could be better right now? How can you make changes to make it happen?

Health	Happiness	Purpose

Use the reflective questions during the reset to recalibrate and get back on track to maintaining a *Principal in Balance* status. These questions are great to reflect on and gentle reminders for ensuring you are ready for upcoming stressful seasons.

Doing the Homework: Practice Not Perfection

When you are operating at a higher-than-optimal level of stress, what can you let go of to regain rest?

What can you do to find time to reset?

CHAPTER 3

Focus on Your Feelings

Don't let your *languishing* cause you to *lash out.*

#PrincipalinBalance

We are really good at naming things in education. A new curriculum, a new approach to teaching, a new special education category or identification of a specific special education population—we are on it. Enter any kindergarten classroom and you will see labels for everything in the room. So why, if we are so good at naming and labeling things for students, do we not do that for ourselves?

Feel · ing \ 'fē-liŋ: an emotional state or reaction

Too often as adults we don't take the time to identify our feelings, we just try to push through, stuff them in, or attempt to ignore them. This response to a feeling, especially when in stressful situations, results in negative emotional or physical responses. By ignoring them we also don't give ourselves the time to really reflect and identify what we are feeling so we can work on why we are feeling this way and how to move forward.

When we struggle to accurately define our feelings, our emotional health and our overall well-being are impacted. We can't just be fine all the time.

Lucky for us there is a growing body of research out there about healthy workplaces and resilient people we can bring into education and use for ourselves and each other. The importance of this topic and the need for the conversations have to move past sharing an article at a staff meeting. It needs to be included in our professional development, providing time and space to have conversations with each other, and locations that allow for staff to talk about this topic.

In the book *Permission to Feel,* Marc Bracket explains that labeling emotions accurately increases self-awareness and helps us communicate emotions effectively, reducing misunderstanding in social interactions (Brackett 2019). The trouble with this in the workplace is making the time and making yourself vulnerable enough to be honest about how you are feeling. We often go to our staple emotion response when coworkers ask how we are doing: fine, okay, good. But none of those words are actual emotions. According to the Juno Institute and the Wheel of Human Emotions, there are 6 core emotions: love, fear, anger, sadness, surprise, and joy. And under each of those 6 emotions are another 15 that go deeper and are more specific about identifying true feelings in the moment. Reflecting on your feelings and becoming more specific with them, you can really focus on why you are feeling what you are feeling. Is it a desirable or undesirable feeling, and what is this doing to your current energy level (and mood)?

Take a moment. What are you thinking about right now? What recent interaction is bothering you? Was it a short response to a person asking a question? Was it imploding on your spouse at home about a household chore not being done? Or are you rehashing a conversation with a parent, coworker, or supervisor that has left you off-kilter? Are you sad or, more specifically, regretful for the short response you gave to a simple question from a coworker? Are you feeling angry, or maybe more so exasperated because of the multiple times you have asked for something to be completed and it still isn't done? Are you surprised or more personally shocked at being on the receiving end of that recent conversation that didn't go according to plan? By focusing on specific feelings, you can find ways to respond, regulate, and articulate how to move forward, and not continue to rehash the past.

So, let's create a vocabulary that honors the importance of this work and find ways to incorporate it in our daily lives. And let's take the first step toward pushing past "I'm fine."

YOU CAN'T BE FINE ALL THE TIME

That "f" word. And not the one I hear in the halls of the middle school, or sometimes written on the bathroom stalls. This "f" word is more dismissive and damaging to those who say it. It can come with hidden guilt and shame for not being happy all the time. Not finding joy in the daily disasters our classrooms and home lives can be in isn't a reason to cover it up with the "f" word. It just isolates and silos us more from each other and from those who might be able to help.

Spoiler alert: when people say they are "fine," often they are not.

So how do you move past the "f" word? It takes time, patience, and a willingness to sit with someone to help them go a little deeper as well.

- **Be invested.** If you want to support a workplace culture that pushes past surface level responses, you have to be ready to invest the time to listen to others. Make a point to stop in and talk to the person at a time that works for them, not just you.

Maybe it is their prep period, maybe they come to school early or stay later. Whenever it is, make sure they have the time, space, and comfortable environment to dig into their own feelings. *Hey, I was wondering if you had some time this week to talk? I have noticed in the halls that your interactions with students have shifted a little bit. It seems like you have a lot on your plate and something on your mind. I really care about you and want to help—could we connect sometime? It can be before/after school or at lunch. We could go for a walk or meet up in your classroom. Again, my intentions are to make sure you are doing okay and to be available if you need anything or just want to talk.*

- **Be detailed.** For some, this new way of reflecting on our own feelings will be hard and, just like us, they may not have the vocabulary to identify what they are really feeling. Having a visual like the Wheel of Human Emotions, or another way to reference different feelings, may be helpful.

  Don't be afraid to give an outside perspective to a situation. If you saw an interaction between the person and a student, it is okay to ask them what they were feeling at the time. For example, you might start out with: How are you doing? No, really. And if the response is, I'm *fine*, try something like this: *I am wondering how you are feeling right now? I ask because earlier today I saw you with a student. It seemed like they were asking a question, but the response that you gave was pretty loud and the student looked a little stunned by your response. Would you be willing to talk me through what happened during the interaction? Or what you were feeling before it started? Is something else going on right now that might have caused the heightened response? Is there anything I can do to help?*

  By walking someone through seeing a situation with a neutral set of eyes, you can help them see outside themselves and give a different perspective. The caution with this work is not to be judgmental, but objective. Describe what you saw and attempt to give emotional words to help be more specific, but not critical. The next step will help with that bridge to openness.

- **Be vulnerable.** One of the best ways to help others start to identify their emotions is by you modeling it first. I have gotten better at sharing my examples first to build trust and diminish the sense of expected perfection in this profession. Let's all admit it right here—we have all been the sender of communication that caused the receiver to have a negative emotional reaction. It could be at home, at school, or in a social setting. My tone, my body language, or my words have hurt others.

In these open and honest conversations, your vulnerability may provide the other person with trust to share their own emotions, and permission to not be perfect or pretend anymore. This could look like sharing your own experiences that might align with what the other person is going through. *Hey, I want you to know I am not checking up on you but checking in. A few years ago, when we were going through a really tough time at home, I noticed if I was upset from an interaction at home right before I left, I could "leak" out emotions on my students in the classroom. In reflection, it was rarely about the question they were asking at the time; it was more about my lack of emotional regulation before I walked in the classroom door.*

- **Be ready.** If you work within a culture where emotions are not regularly discussed, the first few times you start to ask these questions you might be shut down or shut out. Don't stop trying. Building a school culture that values people before their professional title takes time and investment. You might ask the same person three times to connect before they finally take you up on it. This work requires you to be flexible with your time and ready when others are ready to talk or share.

  Please know it is okay and necessary to still have your own boundaries on these conversations. Being invested in another person does not have to be at your expense. If they want to meet after school that day and you had plans to go to your child's event, it is okay (and essential) to let the person know that tonight doesn't work but that you still want to connect. *I am so happy you reached out and I want to sit down and connect. Tonight, I have plans to attend Kenny's swim meet, but I am free after work this Thursday or Friday. Would either of these days work? Thank you for understanding that I want to be fully present for our conversation, which means I need to make sure I have no other commitments that would conflict with our time.*

With these actions in practice, you will cultivate a culture that values the adult's feelings and mental well-being as much as the students and families you serve.

A NEW WAY TO FEEL ABOUT HOW WE ARE FEELING

Adam Grant (2021) published a piece in the *New York Times* that helped to bring this feeling to the forefront of conversations. It wasn't burnout—we still had energy. It wasn't depression—we didn't feel hopeless. We just felt somewhat joyless and aimless. It turns out there's a name for that: languishing.

Languish \ 'laŋ-gwish: to become dispirited

As educators and leaders, I think we have all been in a season of languishing. A time when we are not sure if what we are doing is making a difference. A period of life when the work isn't as enjoyable as the effort we put into it. Grant goes on to say that languishing is in between depression and flourishing. In other words, it is the absence of well-being when your resilience reservoir needs to kick in and help you back up and out of this state before you spiral into depression or anxiety.

Strategies and supports that build a resilience reservoir include staying focused on a goal, being grounded in purpose, finding clarity in your work, and setting aside focused time for projects and plans.

Staying focused can be hard when we are not 100%, but also not in a space where we are completely spent. I think about seasons when my self-care was not optimal, but not because of a major injury or illness, but rather a lack of focus and purpose. Solutions to refocusing will be addressed in the work around self and soul care. But remember, if you are struggling to regain your why, you might need to spend a little more time planning how you will work to get it back.

Focused time is essential when you are less motivated than normal to get to work. As an educator there is no better month for this than May. When you are having a hard time staying on track, finding less energy to accomplish things, and stress levels are on the rise, try this strategy: purpose, pause, and praise.

- **Purpose in planning:** May for me is exhausting. It is the end of the marathon of the school year and always seems to be sprinkled with extra evening commitments for school as well as spring/summer activities kicking in for my own children. From track meets to spring basketball practices in a neighboring town, I seem to be gone more than I am home. These are all for good reason—but all the more reason I have to be intentional with my time.

To create more purpose and accountability in my days, each Sunday I complete a weekly preview in my Full Focus Planner. I make sure to outline how many nights I have family commitments, so I know what I need to say no to at work to make sure I get the rest I need to have the bandwidth to be ready for the next day.

- **Pause in the pace:** During the month of May, it can feel like an exhausting sprint. You may feel frustrated you didn't finish with the energy to do your best work. In the race to get grades done, prepare next year's schedules, write final newsletters, and conduct assemblies, it is easy to run on autopilot. You get so caught up in the fast pace that when you look back, you don't remember many of the details.

  The danger of pushing instead of pausing is you lose the chance to do your best work. Think about when you are tired, stressed, and frustrated. Was the email you wrote and sent your best? Was the interaction with the student or staff member tougher than needed? Self-regulation means taking the time necessary to be ready for what comes next, and sometimes that will require you to slow your pace instead of pushing through.

  During this season make sure you have more margin in your day than normal. Leave work at a reasonable hour at least three days a week, and when you do leave, leave work at work. No after-hours emails. Modeling boundaries helps to give others explicit permission to do the same.

- **Praise in the process:** Too often we race through the day so that we don't take the time to give others, or ourselves, the recognition we need. As educators, we can focus on the negative noise and feedback more than the great things we do every day. Flipping the switch and learning how to focus more on the good will pay off in building resilience for the next few weeks ahead.

  An activity we completed in May during team meetings helped ground us in this process. We took the time to write words of affirmation to each other and then we each read them aloud. Following the activity, we reinforced the importance of prioritizing the compliments from those we care about most, and to stop giving time and space in our minds for the complaints and criticism from those in the cheap seats.

As you prepare for a season of languishing, or if you are coming out of one, remember it is okay to not be okay, but it isn't okay to stay there forever.

GRACE AND SPACE FOR EMOTIONS

As a principal who lives and leads in the small community of Austin, Minnesota, I have had the blessing to see many of my students throughout their educational career. From Head Start to high school, I have seen them through many circumstances and situations. I even pride myself on being a "Grand Principal," a term I made up meaning I was the parent's principal and now I serve as their child's principal.

So, when a student is having a meltdown, I might have more insight, history, and information than others. For the past five years, a certain month of the year triggers two siblings as the anniversary of finding their parents deceased. Growth in the middle grades sometimes doesn't show the full story of the student starting in kindergarten with no language and a wide range of physical behaviors. This history helps support students navigate the trauma triggers as they occur, and give teams insight into difficult seasons and reasons why. So adults, why do we feel shame sharing our dark spots? Not to seek sympathy but to build empathy in our own circumstances and find ways to support each other?

For me, December is hard. While most are getting excited about family gatherings, special activities, and extended time away from work, I am working hard in the opposite direction: seeking routine, keeping my nucleus tight, and Kleenex closer. In the adoption circles, the day you and your child come home is called a "Gotcha Day"; while that is a popular term, we refrain from that and consider it our son's "Adoption Day." The day we waited for, fought to get, and one that threw me into the deepest depression I may ever experience. December is difficult. Even a decade later, there are emotions that bubble up. Recognize that just because I have different feelings than others is not a reason for guilt, shame, or blame. It is an opportunity to name them and feel comfortable sharing with others why our family traditions might look different than most.

We as a family tend to keep holiday decorations at a more minimal level than going overboard in every room. We also hold tight to at least two or three "normal" nights at home during December. We choose to say no to more holiday parties and extended family events so we have sacred time and space for quiet, calm recalibration. One tradition we hold sacred is the remembrance and celebration of that Adoption Day. Every year on or right around the original day we came home, we drive to the same airport and take a family picture in the same space. And each year that picture is a focal point in our family albums and bookmarks the end of one year and the start of the next.

Sharing this story with the staff I serve and other administrators in my district is not meant to gain sympathy for our family circumstances. Lesson learned: don't be afraid to let others in because you will need someone to lean on and help.

FROM FINE TO FLOURISH

We started this chapter out with the dreaded "f" word. The one most used in the lounge, hallways, or in an effort to check in on someone when we really are trying to check off the box. We all know what depression, anguish, frustration, and now languishing feel like, but what about flourishing?

Flour · ish \ 'flə-rish: a period of thriving

According to Merriam-Webster, flourishing is marked by vigorous and healthy growth. If you look up flourishing on Dictionary.com (*Flourishing Definition & Meaning*, n.d.), it adds growing vigorously, thriving; prosperous. However you define it, sign me up for feeling this way more often.

The first step toward moving
into a state of flourish is to set your sights on it.

#PrincipalinBalance

What do you want to do? And how can you do it well? And, most importantly, what needs to come off your plate so the work you do is fulfilling, enjoyable, and obtainable?

In future chapters, we will start the process of moving into more flourishing and less fine in our lives. To accomplish this transition, we need to be intentional with what we want to accomplish, and okay with saying no to

others on the things that will take time away from us, our purpose, and the goals we set for ourselves. So, spend a few minutes thinking about what flourishing might look like in the following environments:

- What would growing and thriving look like in my school or classroom?
- How could I have more energy to thrive when I am home with my family?
- Where can I put time into my day to include more activities in life that will help me stay focused on my purpose and have time and bandwidth for my goals?

Reflecting regularly on these questions will help you grow in your understanding of flourish and find ways to work strategies for ongoing success in this area every day.

NAMING IT AND TAMING IT

When you can identify what you are feeling, there is a better chance you can seek the right course of treatment to move from one end of the spectrum to the other. When you don't identify correctly and just start pushing through without support, well, that is when you can lash out.

In this chapter, we have talked about the importance of feelings, and how to work with, or through, them. Moving into the next segments of the book, we will work through activities, exercises, and ideas that will help us move from just fine to flourishing. Some of these will be common sense and easy to incorporate, others might be more challenging.

You probably didn't pick this book up because you are flourishing and resilient in work and life 100% of the time. Chances are you hadn't even really thought that much about your feelings, actions, and activities and how they can impact your quality of life. Moving into how to become a *Principal in Balance* doesn't require you to have Principal in your work title, but it does require you to take the lead on your life and take control of what consumes your mind, time, and what might come out of your mouth.

GENTLE REMINDER: THERE IS NO FAULT IN HAVING FEELINGS

Don't be afraid to acknowledge your feelings. By identifying what is going well and how that makes you feel is as important as naming how you feel when things are right. Once you can articulate your emotions, you can find ways to stay in that flow and flourish or use activities from your resiliency reserves to shift your current mood from fine or frustrated toward flourishing.

Do the Homework: Finding More Flourishing in Our Days

What types of activities bring you to a flow of flourishing?

How can you find time to incorporate more of these activities into a regular routine?

What needs to go so you can stay more in a flow?

CHAPTER 4

Everything in Moderation

Do it perfect? or Do it well.

The shiny new thing syndrome. We see a new trend or technique, a way of doing something we haven't thought of before and we drop everything, throw all the things out, and race after this new magical fix. For those of us who are driven by internal or external motivations, we can throw ourselves into the new thing so deep we can lose sight of everything else.

mod · er · ate \ 'mä-d(ə-)rət avoiding extremes of behavior or expression: observing reasonable limits

As someone who loves learning and attending conferences, I always was excited to attend the National Principal Conferences in the summer. However, the staff I serve were always scared. Oh my, who is she going to be bringing back to speak, what new things are we going to do, and how much time will it take? Early on in my career, I would come back with pages of ideas, initiatives, and things we could change or tweak. I soon realized doing all the things on all the pages was not going to be sustainable or successful.

For some of us, the "going all in" also can impact our relationships and life at home. Think about New Year's resolutions (we have all tried them at least once). I will exercise more, eat less, spend more time at home, do more activities with family, read more, watch TV less, social media fasts, or meal plan more. We can go into these resolutions with 110% energy, not realizing we might have only a 35% capacity to achieve them in the long run. This mathematical imbalance ends up leaving everyone frustrated and unfulfilled with yet another resolution dead in the water.

The previous three chapters have given us a case for why this work is essential and necessary. This chapter will prepare us for the work ahead by this golden rule:

PICK ONE THING AND DO IT WELL

Chances are you have taken on too much during a point in your life. Maybe it was saying yes to coaching your child's soccer team while you were already layered with committees and extra responsibilities at work. Or maybe you decided to go back to school, but instead of reassessing your current commitments and taking something off your plate, you just rearranged it all to fit one more thing into your days and weeks. Regardless of how it started, without re-evaluating all the "other duties as assigned" in life, I can guarantee they will overwhelm you or run you down. Even worse, you may get to a point where instead of wanting to do it well, you just want to get it done.

> Don't get to the point where instead of wanting to do it well, you just want to get it done.
>
> *#PrincipalinBalance*

Before you start deleting things from your calendar and saying no to anything and everything, it is important to get grounded in what your schedule and your life currently look like. The best way to assess the bandwidth and boundaries in your work and life is to first start with your calendar.

ASSESSING YOUR SCHEDULE

To identify if you are doing too much, you have to take inventory of what you are currently doing to see if anything can just be delegated, deleted, or just something you can be finished with moving forward.

Try this activity to assess what your schedule currently looks like. Take the next 10 minutes to map out your week. Write down any meetings, pickup/drop-offs from school, family activities, and courses you teach or take. An example might look like this:

Sunday	Monday	Tuesday	Wednesday	Thursday	Friday	Saturday
9-12 Church		Bus Duty/Parent Drop-off 8:00-8:20				Long Run
	Lunch Sup. 11:50-12:50	Building Leadership 9-11	District Leadership 9-12	Classroom Visits 9-11	Lunch Sup. 12:50-1:50	
		Isaiah Soccer 6-7:30	Manny Basketball 6:30-9:30	Mastermind 7:00-9:00		
		Bus Duty 3:25-3:35				

If you can do a second round, look at your online calendar/paper planner and think about the following questions as you brain dump your day:

- What does your daily schedule look like from the moment you wake up until you go to sleep?
- What titles do you hold during your day at work and home?
- What are your yearly activities that you are involved with (i.e., soccer parent, committee chairs, team leader, summer school lead)?

Now take 10 more minutes to answer the following question:

- What would you do (hobbies, activities, interests) if you had everything done?

Once you have this brain dump completed, it is time to take inventory of everything you wrote down and start to categorize these activities, roles, and titles in life into defined areas of your life.

In the book *Balance Like a Pirate* (Cabeen et al. 2018), we speak of balance as quadrants in life. And while we recognize not all quadrants are equal, it is essential to have time and activities in each of these areas. The quadrants are defined as:

- **Personal:** Things that make you who you are outside of the "titles" you hold.
- **Positional:** Defining what you need to do to be successful in your day job and setting boundaries around the rest to have a life.
- **Professional:** How you are finding ways and making time to continue to learn and grow in your profession.
- **Passions:** What do you do for fun, or better yet what would you do for free? Identifying your hobbies and ideas of things to do for fun will allow you to have time to engage in these activities on a more regular basis.

Personal	Professional
Positional	Passions

When I work with coaching clients, I ask them to think about all the things they do within a day, a week, a month, and write them down. Then we transfer those activities into the chart by area they fit in. In my years of doing this activity, two things have been clear: we do way too much to fit in the chart (positional), and we don't do enough for ourselves (personal and passion).

The next step of this process is to find a way to take a few things off the chart before we add more activities or commitments.

GOING BIG WILL CAUSE YOU TO JUST GO HOME

So here is where moderation comes in—when you see everything that is written down, you can see that it is unrealistic for anyone to accomplish it all. To live as a *Principal in Balance*, you to have to recognize that the idea of doing it all has to be done. Saying yes to everyone and everything means you are going to do nothing well and feel more depleted, worn down, and burned out than ever before.

The idea of *doing it all*,
has to *be done*.

#PrincipalinBalance

Has the compelling reason for moderation set in yet? Are you ready to start taking things off your plate and being content with a new narrative of doing fewer things well instead of doing it all awfully?

Let's go back to that list within the framework. What category has the most activities listed within it? Start looking at this list hard with the lens of these questions:

- What activities in this category are essential to my life, or my career? *Circle these.*
- Do I absolutely have to do this thing? Is this an essential part of my job, or my job description? *Circle these.*
- What activities in this category have I carried from one job position to the next? *Cross out.*
- What activities should I say no to but feel bad about not doing them? *Cross out.*

If you have any activities not sorted yet, ask these questions:

- If I stopped doing this thing, what would happen?
- Who else can do this task?

Reviewing the framework with this lens is hard. Recognizing we might be doing things we don't really need to do is one thing; taking the step to stop altogether is another challenge (and one we will get to later).

BABY STEPS TO START BALANCING

While this process might feel frustrating, overwhelming, confusing, or scary, the product you will complete will be worth it: a more balanced life with bandwidth to do the things you want to do and the ability to establish boundaries to say no to everything else.

So, let's get into the "one" thing. In each of the quadrants, identify one activity or action you want to get better at within the next six to eight weeks. Here are a few examples you can draw from:

Personal	Professional
Get 12,000 steps in a day.	Read/listen to 1 podcast or article a week on middle school brain development.
Positional	**Passions**
Leave work by 4:30 p.m. 3 nights a week.	Write a blog post 1 time per month.

By taking the time to identify a few small things to start balancing your work and your life, you will see quick wins and be motivated to continue. As educators, we are used to serving everyone else. At times, sacrificing ourselves, our time, our resources, and our energy leaves us depleted for the things we need and want to accomplish.

Because we are making such hard turns in our prior practices, taking it slow and being intentional are essential so we don't slip up, or slip back into our old ways.

In James Clear's book *Atomic Habits* (Clear 2018, p. 162), he explores the impact of the Two-Minute Rule. He notes that even when you know you should start small, it's easy to start too big. Learning how to break up a big project, goal, new habit, or activity you want to pursue into small steps, objectives, or measurable outcomes can build quick wins, small successes, and better buy-in for the long road ahead.

Think about your last New Year's resolution. How long did it last? Did you start out too big, get disappointed, and quit? With the Two-Minute Rule you can effectively start (and sustain) a new habit when it should take less than two minutes to do.

So, let's take our Pick One Thing quadrant framework and add the Two-Minute Rule (TMR) to the process.

Personal	Professional
Get 12,000 steps in a day. TMR: Go for a 2-minute walk during passing time in the halls.	Read/listen to 1 podcast or article a week on middle school brain development. TMR: Print one article a week and read it during classroom observations or student independent work time.
Positional	Passions
Leave work by 4:30 p.m. 3 nights a week. TMR: Put "Work Shut Down Routine" on your calendar for 4:20 p.m. every day.	Write a blog post 1 time per month. TMR: Freewrite for 2 minutes every week on a subject.

By breaking down the habits you want to start into smaller steps, there is a higher chance you will see success much sooner. This is instead of trying to do it all—all at once—and quitting before you really got started.

Clear goes on to state the golden rule of creating habits: mastering the art of showing up (Clear 2018, p. 164). More than half the battle will be prioritizing time for yourself, your well-being, and the development of a self-care and soul-care plan that is reasonable, achievable, and sustainable. By showing up to the four quadrants you are saying "yes" to yourself.

A habit example of this work is my morning routine. For years, I rolled out of bed and began racing through my day. Too often I hit snooze five times or more, so I was already behind before I started. Before I did anything else, I looked at my email, calendar, and social media feeds. I stressed about what I needed to get done prior to making my morning coffee, or because I spent too much time reading these emails, I missed my morning exercise.

Because I was sleeping in, I also was trying to get myself ready alongside my two elementary-aged boys. My husband was out the door to work before they were up, so most days were a power struggle for all of us, and some days one of us was in tears before we left.

I look back now on how our mornings ran and can't believe what a difference adding 30 minutes in the morning made.

When I started blogging, a friend recommended a book that could help me find consistent time to write during my week. *The Miracle Morning for Writers: How to Build a Writing Ritual That Increases Your Impact and Your Income* by Hal Elrod and Steve Scott was more than a way to find time to write; it gave me a system to give me more time in the mornings for myself overall. In the book, they highlight the six-step morning routine using what are called Life S.A.V.E.R.S.: **silence, affirmations, visualization, exercise, reading, and scribing** (Corder and Scott 2016). Since starting my morning rituals, I have modified this routine to better fit my lifestyle.

Jessica's Morning Routine

5:15 a.m.	Wake up! I leave my phone in the bathroom so I can't hit snooze.
5:20 a.m.	Coffee, take the dog outside quickly, and get out my Bible study or devotional.
5:30–5:50 a.m.	Morning devotional (5 minutes). Morning gratitude journal (5 minutes). Chapter in one book (10 minutes).
5:50–6:30 a.m.	Morning exercise (4 days per week). • 30-minute run • 30-minute bike • 30-minute walk with dog Writing time (1 day per week). • Blog, book writing, article prep.
6:30–7:15 a.m.	Wake up boys and get ready for work. • Listen to a podcast while getting ready. • Check in on teenagers to make sure they are moving and have things ready for school.
7:15–7:30 a.m.	Make a smoothie and head to work.

While this might look intense at first, this has been a work in progress for 10 years. When I first started, I focused on consistent self-care time (exercise and quiet time); as I built a stronger routine, I added soul-care time in as well (devotional, gratitude, reading). Now this is such a habit that even if I wanted to sleep in, I can't.

Key to this morning routine is one thing: don't answer emails. Sustaining this routine means setting firm boundaries up front. Your time is where your mind goes, and if the first thing you focus on every day is work, how do you prioritize time for yourself?

Getting back to James Clear's Two-Minute Rule, look at your weekly calendar and daily routines. Are there incremental ways to start moving toward this routine in two minutes or less?

Maybe you already get up early. What if your first step was to stop checking email or social media? That gives you at least 2, if not 10 minutes back.

What is one thing you would like to do more regularly to start your day?

- Exercise
- Devotional
- Read
- Meditate
- Journal

Choose one of the above activities and incorporate the Two-Minute Rule (examples below):

- Exercise: *Set out clothes the night before.*
- Devotional: *Have a devotional prepared and next to the space you will do it the next morning.*
- Read: *Have the book near where you will sit in the morning.*
- Meditate: *Have daily affirmations printed out or in a journal (caution with keeping it on your phone unless you are disciplined enough to not look at other apps, email, etc.).*
- Journal: *Have pens and a journal ready to write in with multiple journal prompts ready to go.*

By breaking down the habits you want to start into small meaningful and actionable items, there is a higher likelihood these habits will become ingrained in your day and then you can stack them later on.

> **GENTLE REMINDER: WHEN YOU THINK YOU HAVE TO DO IT ALL, YOU WILL DO NOTHING WELL.**
>
> When we regularly review our commitments to make sure we have bandwidth in our day, it will impact our overall well-being. If we have a calendar where we honor boundaries that reflect our priorities at work and in life, it won't deplete the resiliency reserves we are building up for times of crisis.

Doing the Homework: Building Your Morning Routine

Create your own Morning Routine using the template below.

Principal in Balance Morning Routine

Activity	Time to Complete

PART II

DREAM BIG

59

Prioritizing Purpose for the Passions in Your Life

WHAT ARE YOUR DREAMS?

If someone asked, could you identify dreams you have for your life? For your vocation? For what you want to be when you grow up? I am in my late 40s and still figuring it out. If you can't identify those dreams, this section is for you and, most importantly, all about you.

Dream:\ 'drēm: a strongly desired goal or purpose

What do you want to accomplish? Is there something you want to do in life and just haven't found time to get it done? What do you want to become, and where are you called to lead? Often we reserve dreaming big for younger generations, the students we teach, our own children, or those we mentor and support. But when we forget to focus on our own dreams, we are not setting a good example for those we mentor. Are you living a life you would want your own children to lead? These chapters will give you the margin and a framework to shift the focus back to you and your dreams.

WHEN WAS THE LAST TIME YOU FOCUSED ON YOUR DREAMS?

This section will help ground us in our goals. So often we go through our day without really reflecting on our purpose and prioritizing the activities and actions that drive us closer to our goals. But before we move forward, we have to identify what we want to be and do in life, and how we want to be remembered after we are gone.

It is one thing to have dreams you want to accomplish. It is another to find the time and margin in your life to achieve these dreams. And while you can't pour from an empty cup, you can't achieve a goal in life without rest, margin, and a plan.

Dreaming big is going to give you the necessary time to pause, rest, and reset to focus on yourself and what you want to accomplish. Going through the prompts will allow you to sit and think about ideas, goals, and dreams you have wanted to accomplish "if only" you had the time. Slowing down and being still provides you with the bandwidth to focus on how you can grow.

In these chapters you will find many examples of how to set goals that provide the flexibility to find one way that works for you and the motivation to not only get it started, but, most importantly, to get it done.

Some of our best dreams occur when we have set optimal conditions in our environment to be ready to receive or see what is ahead. These optimal conditions go back to our developing resiliency reserve lists and the explicit permission to give yourself a pass to rest.

Margin is an uncomfortable concept for some of us. As a driven (a.k.a. workaholic) person, it is hard to shift a perception that going all the time isn't really going to get you anywhere. Setting aside time each week to reflect on the dreams you have set and recalibrating a plan to achieve them requires patience, persistence, and time within your calendar to sit and be with your thoughts. This is contrary to popular culture of racing to the next activity or trying to multitask yourself to death.

HOW WILL I ACCOMPLISH THESE DREAMS?

In these chapters, I will share multiple frameworks I have utilized in different seasons of my life to achieve the dreams and goals I have had. While none of these are one-size-fits-all, I challenge you to land on one to help you achieve a dream you have. Remember James Clear's golden rule: master the art of showing up. So slow down, have a seat, get a paper and pen ready, and get ready to dream.

This is a great start.

CHAPTER 5

Recommitting:
The Essential Three

When you are committed to your calling,
your purpose becomes clearer.

#PrincipalinBalance

Happy New Year! No, don't look at the calendar, or wait to read this until December 31. Spoiler Alert: I love a new year. New school years, new starts to the calendar year, even new school quarters. For me, it is a chance to review, reflect, and recalibrate my purpose, revisit my goals (both personal and professional), and renew my commitment to my callings.

For some of us, we do this regularly. For others, we haven't thought about this in a while. Why do you do what you do? What brought you to this moment in time and your current occupation in work and life? Before we set our exciting and achievable goals for the next season of life, it is important to be grounded in a foundation of why we do what we do and who we want to become. In other words, knowing exactly why we pull into that parking spot at work or park in the garage at night and what we bring to elevate our work every day.

This chapter is foundational to becoming a *Principal in Balance*. It has been said many ways, but when you have an identified calling, you can move through your day with more intention and direction. A calling grounds you in a purpose for leading in life and at work. And the alignment of your calling with your purpose and work in work and life can help ground you in purpose and be the foundation for goal-setting.

pur · pose \ 'pər-pəs: a subject under discussion or an action in course of execution

Have you ever started driving to one destination but by habit or routine you end up somewhere else? For weeks after I switched schools, I would occasionally still slip back into an old habit and end up in my former school's parking lot. I will sometimes head into another room at home looking for one specific thing, but by the time I get there I have forgotten what I was looking for. Or even worse, if I am not focused on what I am saying, I regularly get my boys' names mixed up and it is common for Kenny to be called *Isaiah, Herman . . . wait, Kenny.* These mental slips aren't the sign of dementia or a serious health crisis but are equally important to figure out and fix.

Too often I put my *purpose* on *autopilot.*

#PrincipalinBalance

I run through my day on routine and race through opportunities for meaningful connection or chances to go deeper into a conversation, activity, or event. I have sat through full conversations with another person and not even realized what they said. If I am sitting with my kids and I have my phone out, they always know when I am off in space thinking about what I am seeing, texting, or tweeting.

I am not the unique case here. Unfortunately, I am the norm.

Living well requires you to really lead your life and push pause on autopilot. Shifting away from hurry, hustle, and external praise and gratification requires a consistent, intentional process to course-correct, and ways to ensure checks and balances so you don't slip back into the more familiar routine.

A CALL TO ACTION

To know your direction, you have to know where you are going. Too often we want to achieve something, but don't take the intentional time to specifically lay out three things: what we want to do, why we want to do it, and how we can get it done. And be careful not to mistake your calling for your title.

You don't need a title,
but you do need a purpose.

#PrincipalinBalance

Time and time again I have done this, merging my purpose with my title. When you assume your title is your calling, you will question your foundation when things shift. In my personal life, the disruption in our adoption was a clear example of this as my inner voice told me that if I couldn't adopt, I wouldn't be a good mom. Focusing on the attributes and the gifts you bring to a position, rather than your title, allows you to utilize your resilience reserves when things get hard. By focusing on my abilities to care for and comfort children, I took my calling outside of my role as mom and utilized these talents as an educator, a principal, and a mentor to other children in our community. With this focus I recalibrated and refocused my purpose in life and built back the reserves needed to move forward from that challenging season.

In work, we may all have experienced the overlap of our calling and our positions. This can be tricky when we live in a purpose that is our title, not our intentions. If you became a leader because you want to serve others, you can do that no matter the position. If you became a leader for a paycheck, a positional status change, or to feel important, it will be challenging to live that out every day.

Purpose is a little more general. There may be a lot of us who got into our fields of study and what we do in life for the same reason. Our calling however is more specific. It is the unique contribution you give to your organization and those around you.

Calling \ 'kȯ-liŋ: a strong inner impulse toward a particular course of action especially when accompanied by conviction of divine influence

Realizing your work as a calling over a job or something you do elevates the importance of the work and helps you realize what you can do to contribute to the position you have. And whatever your title is now, if you are living out your calling, don't diminish the work you are doing. You are not "just" anything, you are something—own it and be proud of how you are contributing.

THREE WAYS TO COMMIT TO YOUR CALLING

Calling? Really? But I am just a (insert your title, role at home, etc.). Whatever your title is at home, work, or anywhere else means you can be in the driver's seat of how you do what you do. Thinking of daily tasks and routines as "have to" instead of "get to" changes how you do what you do. This shift in thinking can also recalibrate why you took the position, moved to the new location, or continue in the work you started years ago.

Step 1: Why do you do what you do?

Often, we are too busy to reflect on why we do the work we do. And more often than we like to admit, we focus on the other responsibilities that come along with the work instead of the primary purpose. We get stuck in the procrastinating details so that we lose focus on our ultimate target and goal. For the next 30 minutes take a pause to reflect on the purpose of your current calling.

Take out a piece of paper and a timer. Without any other notifications or distractions, set the timer for 25 minutes and complete at least two of the following prompts:

How do I show up and serve others?

Who is someone I have been able to serve in my calling (work or personal)?

What was I able to contribute?

How does my work benefit others?

I am most happy in my calling when . . .

Finished? What did you learn? Taking intentional time to reflect on the deeper meaning of why you do what you do is essential as we move into step 2 of recommitment and recalibrating our calling. Before we write down our goals, we need to get clear on the connection of how our dreams connect to our calling and align with our purpose.

Before Step 2, finish this sentence:

My purpose in this work (insert title/calling) is to . . .

Got it? Good. I suggest you put this on a post-it note, index card, or screen saver on your phone to remind you on a regular basis of the calling you have committed to.

Step 2: Who benefits from your calling?

In Dr. Amit Sood's book *The Mayo Clinic Guide to Stress-Free Living,* he stresses the importance of seeing what you do as having a deeper meaning than just the title on your door (Sood 2013, p. 200). He continues to build a foundation through the following exercise: Start by identifying people who are positively affected by your efforts. When you realize your work truly touches, directly or indirectly, many people, you may see your work as a calling. Attaching your work to something larger than you can give it a higher meaning.

The exercise is not about humility; it is about specifically identifying the gifts you bring to the work you do while understanding the greater impact your work has on the school, students, and community you serve.

One way to find these skills is to switch positions. Recently I found out I would be transitioning out of my current school assignment to a new one. Sometimes you don't find out about the difference you made until it is time for you to leave.

As I was preparing to leave one position to start another, many staff, students, and parents made a point to congratulate me, and identify what I did to make a difference in their life. Responses ranged from you are always positive, you are visible, you really care about kids, you modeled prioritizing family, you gave us permission to not work all the time, you pushed and challenged us, but also gave us grace if we made mistakes, you cared about all kids, you invested in our families outside of school, you researched . . . every . . . thing . . . we implemented.

In reflecting on these conversations, I was able to answer the questions above more specifically.

Recalibrating and Recommitting to Your Calling

Who benefits from my work?
Students, staff, parents, community partners, coaches, custodians, cafeteria support, liaison officer, teacher leaders wanting to become principals.
What would they say my gifts or talents are within my calling?
Utilizing research to make decisions, being visible in our school, serving in multiple places (bus duty, cafeteria, hallway) while still making time during the day for the operational tasks that need to be done. Prioritizing the person—not the position; caring; positive attitude—specifically when facing adversity; humility—not afraid of admitting mistakes; willingness to give grace when people are struggling; working toward always expecting the best out of everyone.

| Recalibrating and Recommitting to Your Calling |

What would happen if I didn't show up? What would be missing from our school/organization in my absence?
Loud shoes in the hallway ☺
A person vigilant in ensuring all students have access to activities, coursework, and resources regardless of background, language, or experiences.
A leader who works every day to be a better advocate for students, families, and teachers.
Someone who is visible and verbally lets kids know she cares for them.
A leader who prioritizes self-care over the thought of serving others at our own expense.

While I don't encourage you to wait until a job change to reflect on your calling, for me, this was an opportunity to reflect on what I do well, and what comes naturally. Knowing that makes setting reasonable, achievable, and sustainable goals a much simpler and more exciting process.

Step 3: Have patience, stay teachable, and be humble.

Well, this is easy, right? Now that we took the time to recommit to our calling at work and life, we should be able to step forward and live at 100% capacity, today. Slow down. This is not a race to be won, but a chance to live more fulfilled each day.

And even though you have recommitted to a calling, there will still be "additional duties." Those staff meetings, end-of-quarter reports, tasks that prior to this book may have felt like "another thing." With a recommitment to your calling, look at those additional duties and opportunities to enhance your calling. What skills, attributes, or abilities can you uniquely bring to these activities? Just how you show up in those spaces shows others how you feel about what you are doing, and why you are there. Your energy can attract or repel others, so think about how you can shift your behaviors the next time you walk into something you have to do . . . but would rather not do.

As an educator, you learn there is always more to learn. Now that I have tipped the 20-year mark in this work, I realize that education practices, terms, and other things can circle back with new names, applications, and possibilities. Recalibrating your calling requires you to admit that you still have things to learn. Entering the work with this mindset will allow you to go further and have more meaningful applications when you are comfortable asking for help and learning from others.

Feeling brave? Ask a friend, spouse, or even someone who is directly impacted by your work the following questions:

What do I do really well?

If you had to guess, why do I do the work I do?

If there was one thing I could improve upon, what do you think it would be?

Seeking outside perspective gives you a chance to see the blind spots you might otherwise miss. The challenge with this is being receptive to the feedback given. Note to self: if you are not in a head or heart space to hear feedback, don't ask for it. Put a note in this section and come back later when you are ready to receive the information and excited about the opportunity to learn from it.

There is no better place to learn this lesson than in middle school. Middle schoolers are honest, opinionated, and unfiltered. Recommitting to your calling means you will have good and bad days. Just because something doesn't go according to plan doesn't mean you should walk away or quit. See it as a chance to lean in and learn from your mistakes.

This for me shows up when I am not self-regulated when I respond to others. I might be terser, or my inner middle school girl leaks out in an "aggressive-aggressive" remark. Does that mean I should quit my calling and walk away? Probably not. Might it require me to reflect on the interaction and possibly offer an apology? Gulp, yes.

Knowing and applying the ability to stay humble in your learning allows you to grow in meaningful ways without the fear of what you haven't been doing, to what you can start doing now.

SEEKING AND SEEING THE GOOD AND WORTH IN THE WORK

So, you created your calling "card"—the elevator speech about why you do what you do. What skills do you bring to the work, and how do these skills show up for you in healthy ways? We are creating structures to review when needed and reset when required. But what do you do with it?

I have this weird habit of imagining events further down the road. For example, when I was a junior in high school, I was already imagining what my high school graduation would look like. What songs the band would play. I visualized myself standing on stage wearing a cap and gown and singing the national anthem. I have done similar things for other major events in my life like job transitions, awards, vacations, and my wedding (well before I was even engaged).

So how can you imagine the end before you get there with your new-found priority of purpose? And better yet, how do you find grace in the process? In my book *Lead with Grace: Leaning into the Soft Skills of Leadership*, I define grace as "trying something new every day and forgiving yourself along the way" (Cabeen 2019). Using that as a guidepost for goal-setting, instead of focusing on perfection in your goals, allows room for grace in the process. That is why I rarely ever set a goal for 100%. There are too many variables that will come up and, honestly, we beat ourselves up enough in the day-to-day. We can't allow ourselves to have guilt in the process of getting better by setting exciting and achievable goals. So, if you have a goal of not eating after 7 p.m., great. But if you had one of those Tuesdays and it is 7:30 and you haven't eaten all day, grab a salad or something else. Starvation is not an acceptable answer for a day that goes sideways.

Forgiving yourself is one of the hardest things you can do. Think about all the times you forgave others or talked them off a ledge that you would stand on. For example, how often do you tell others "don't worry about it" when they try to apologize to you, but when you need to forgive yourself you keep bringing it up and beating yourself up about it? Try hard, make mistakes, forgive yourself, get back up, and try again.

Gratitude turns what we have into enough.
– Anonymous

#PrincipalinBalance

Being grateful for everything is not easy. At times it can be beyond challenging. But to get through the messy middle of a goal you are trying to achieve, or a challenging season, finding the good in the process is key.

Never in my life did I think I could find something good about the termination of our adoption. We had been to the orphanage, held our son, met his mother, and made a promise to care for him, and then one phone call in mid-August turned our lives upside down. For months I struggled with overwhelming sadness and depression. Getting up and going to work was more than a challenge and sadness seemed to hover over me like a stubborn dark cloud.

However, in that season, there was good with the really, really bad. Friends and family stepped up, and came over with meals and support. My coworkers found ways to encourage and support and create a safe space for me when I would have a meltdown. My spouse and I became much closer in a season that should have separated us. I learned to find joy in serving and supporting others' children to seek fulfillment from what I lost. I smothered my eldest to the point where I am sure he will need therapy as an adult. But looking back, we will know that even when things were not going to our plans, we still cared for him.

Finding ways to seek the good in the bad helps to recalibrate when the calling you thought you had runs off course or stalls out for a while.

GENTLE REMINDER: REMEMBER YOUR CALLING IS NOT TIED TO A TITLE

Stay away from making the connection that you are your position, not your purpose in life or calling in work. When you don't stop to cultivate the skills of who you are and how you have gotten to this point, you lose the opportunity to build the resiliency reserves needed for when jobs change, life circumstances are disrupted, or a period of life has you calling your plans, purpose, and calling into question.

By focusing on the skills that make you good at what you do and uniquely qualified to try something new, you won't waver as much when hard things happen.

Doing the Homework: Create Your Calling Card

Using these prompts, create a two- or three-sentence calling card for work and life.

- I am good at (insert role) because I bring these skills to the (role).

- I enjoy (insert role) because of (insert actions, activities, or ways you authentically serve).

CHAPTER 6

Resetting: Creating a Goal Framework

Productivity means nothing without purpose.

So, you want to achieve your goals? We all enter goal-setting and implementation wide-eyed and optimistic about success. However, without paying attention to what you are planning to accomplish is important in the long-term success of what you set out to accomplish.

productive\ prə-'dək-tiv: having the quality or power of producing especially in abundance

We all have power to be productive; we just might not want, or know how, to use it. Having power means having the *will*power to walk away from something we want to do, when we know it won't serve in the work we have to do.

. . . Watching Netflix versus reading a book.

. . . Scrolling social media versus spending time meal planning and preparing the family calendar for the week.

. . . Answering emails all day versus shutting down notifications and serving students in the lunchroom, or better yet, eating lunch with other teachers and support staff.

I have listed a few but I think we all have kryptonite that dysregulates us and weakens our willpower.

So how can you develop the discipline to build back willpower in the day and be more productive? Building willpower means you regulate impulsive desires, or as I call it the "fun" stuff. Yes, binge watching Netflix might be more fun than organizing your closet and cleaning out/up old clothes to donate, but what will make you feel better later? Sleeping in can feel good in the moment, but later in the day the guilt will sink in of the run or walk you missed in the morning.

The definition of productive has a final word in it that we tend to leave off when we are assessing our success or building up to doing something new or different: abundance. Producing something is different than abundantly producing something. Abundant to me requires energy, stamina, a plan, and, most importantly, a purpose.

If you are going to do something important to you that will contribute to your work, life, family, shouldn't you do that something . . . well?

Setting goals is important but ensuring you have the time and energy to achieve them is essential.

#PrincipalinBalance

For example, while writing this book I had lofty ideas that I also would start running again, I would spend more dedicated time with the boys, and I would realign our school's strategic plan. I was thrown an unexpected curveball in the form of a new position. Suddenly, the goals I had set out to achieve felt overwhelming and suffocating. And they should have.

Doing a few things well is much better than doing a lot with less energy and effort. To do a few things abundantly well, I had to pause and pivot a few of my other goals. The strategic plan revision turned into an end-of-the-year reflection for the new leader. Running turned into run/walks when I could fit them into my schedule, with no races planned until the book was finished and into edits.

So, let's take a goal audit here and see where we can find abundance, and where we can pause or pivot a few other goals, activities, or interests.

What I had planned to do for the next nine weeks:	What I need to do for the next nine weeks:

What can you **pivot?**

If you have run into a busy season, see if there is anything on the list you can shift in a different direction. Maybe it means delegating it to someone else, or getting it done in a different way.

What can you **pause?**

Okay, three months ago that seemed like a great goal. Then X happened, Y is coming up, and you are afraid to see what Z will be! Pausing something isn't a failure, but a deeper desire to do whatever you set out to do well. You are just waiting for a better time to start it.

What can be **planned** for down the road?

When reflecting on purposeful goal-setting, maybe something you had thought to start now seems better to be paired with something down the road. Going back to school for additional degrees, certificates, and licenses can fall into this line of thinking. When you are already working on a major milestone, it is okay to reprioritize other goals for a time later down the road. Acknowledging when you don't have the bandwidth isn't a sign of failure, it is a sign of waiting to fulfill the goal when you have the abundance of time, resources, etc., to do so.

What is the one thing you want to accomplish with **abundant purpose?**

Saving the best for last. Reflect on what you have pivoted, paused, pushed away, and planned for later. You should be left with a few things you want to do, and can do, really well.

It seems counterproductive and certainly counterintuitive to slow down when you feel so busy, but prioritizing your time and setting out to work on the right goals will help you with the rest of your days.

It is hard to be proud of something you have accomplished if you didn't set out to achieve it in the first place. Throwing darts at a proverbial board and hoping one sticks isn't a sign of long-term success or abundance in the work. It is a symptom of the exhausted, have-it-all-be-it-all-for-everyone attitude we have tried to live up to, and failed at, for years.

Have you ever gotten to the end of a busy day, one in which you crossed a lot of things off your task list, attended a lot of meetings, met with a lot of people, but didn't get anything done?

We are so used to prioritizing business and priding ourselves on getting a lot done that sometimes we neglect to stop, slow down, and focus on the most important goals in our lives.

SET SPECIFIC GOALS AND REALIZE RESULTS

In this chapter, we take all the learning and practice and put it into action. We will look at a variety of ways to focus on a goal, find a framework that works for you, and put it into action.

goal:\ 'gōl : the end toward which effort is directed

There are so many different frames, rules, and ways to set goals. If you already use something that works, keep using it. I will share just a few more well-known frameworks. Remember, you aren't looking for a perfect solution, just one that can start pushing you forward.

SMART Framework

This is a popular framework utilized when setting goals for Individual Educational Plans in schools (IEP). The acronym breakdown looks like this:

- **S**pecific: Narrow in focus.
- **M**easurable: Evidence that shows forward motion toward goal achievement.
- **A**ttainable: Is this within your reach?
- **R**elevant: Will this help you grow? Is this important to your calling?
- **T**imebound: When will this be accomplished?

The focus of the SMART framework is to help you get clear on what you are trying to accomplish, how long it will take, and what success would look like. So, let's put this framework into action:

Immediate need: *My schedule is so crazy, and I am tired at the end of the day. Most days I put prepackaged food in the microwave for the family or get takeout. I also notice my soda consumption during the day is going up, which leaves me more tired and less likely to cook when I get home. My spouse is more than willing to help but does better with a plan in place and responsibilities divided based upon what activities are going on after school.*

Personal goal: *By the end of the quarter, I will have a weekly routine set to eat healthier by planning out meals every week and drinking more water and less soda during the workday.*

Specific	Eat less junk food and drink more water.
Measurable	Weekly meal plans, drink more water, drink less soda.
Attainable	Schedule weekly meal planning/grocery shopping.
Relevant	Eating better will result in better health and wellness for myself and family. Meal planning will also help our finances by thinking ahead and not going out to eat so much.
Timebound	By the end of the quarter the habit will be built to stack upon later.

Immediate need: *I am noticing that my day runs me. I am putting out fires most of the day and neglecting the paperwork and emails filling up my inbox and desk. For most of the year I pull a second shift and work at night after everyone is in bed. I feel frustrated and discouraged I have no downtime at night, and it seems my job is a 24/7 commitment. With younger kids at home, I really want to be present for them at night, and not panicked by what I still need to do when they go to bed.*

Professional goal: *By the end of the week, I will set up regular batching and mega-batching sessions for paperwork and email tasks during my workday so I can leave work at work and be more present at home with my family.*

Specific	Stop taking work home. Find ways in the workday to answer email and complete paperwork.
Measurable	How many nights am I taking things home? How many nights am I shutting it all off?
Attainable	Mega-batching big projects and daily-batching emails.
Relevant	By setting limits on the workday, I'm creating a margin to have a life outside of my job and return to work the next day rested and ready to go again.
Timebound	By scheduling batching sessions daily and weekly, I will have time to catch up on work while still being available in classrooms and for families.

SMARTER Framework

This framework is grounded in Michael Hyatt's work. In his book *Your Best Year Ever,* he stresses the importance of the next two letters of SMART—Exciting and Risky (Hyatt, 2018). Exciting goals drive motivation and persistence, even in the face of obstacles (like two teachers out sick with no subs). Along with Relevant, the other "R" in the SMARTER framework is risky. Risky goals inspire out-of-the-box thinking and require growth and unconventional thinking. As educators, we are recognizing the need to incorporate self-care and soul-care in our daily lives—that is a risk worth taking.

So, let's add the E and R to our previous goals and see what it looks like now:

Specific	Eat less junk food and drink more water.
Measurable	Weekly meal plans, drink more water, drink less soda.
Attainable	Schedule weekly meal planning/grocery shopping.
Relevant	Eating better will result in better health and wellness for myself and family. Meal planning will also help our finances by thinking ahead and not going out to eat so much.
Timebound	By the end of the quarter, the habit will be built to stack upon later.
Exciting	**Incorporating healthier habits will help me have the energy I need to spend more enjoyable time with family and find margin to start exercising more regularly.**
Risky	**Here is the deal, if I don't start making changes now, my long-term health and happiness will be in jeopardy, which is not something I am willing to risk.**

Specific	Stop taking work home. Find ways in the workday to answer email and complete paperwork.
Measurable	How many nights am I taking things home? How many nights am I shutting it all off?
Attainable	Mega-batching big projects and daily-batching emails.
Relevant	By setting limits on the workday, I am creating a margin to have a life outside of my job and return to work the next day rested and ready to go again.
Timebound	By scheduling batching sessions daily and weekly, I will have time to catch up on work, while still being available in classrooms and for families.
Exciting	**Wait, what . . . by doing this I can enjoy my job *and* have a life? Yes, sign me up!**
Risky	**Setting boundaries between work and home means I have to stick with them. If I don't honor my batching sessions, I will get behind on work and miss deadlines or be unable to respond to communication in a timely manner.**

OKRs

In *Measure What Matters*, John Doerr lays out another framework for goal setting and achievement. In this framework, you set out with Objectives and Key Results (OKRs). These are utilized within organizations such as Intel, Google, Remind, and many more.

An objective is what is to be achieved. This is concrete, action-oriented, and inspirational. Key results monitor how to get to the objective. These are specific, time-bound, aggressive, and yet realistic (Doerr 2018, p. 7).

In action, OKRs are quick, visual, and can build on the success of each key result, leading you closer to achieving the objective. Here are a few examples of what OKRs look like in action.

Objective: Have more time for my family.

Key Results:
- Leave work by 5 p.m. three nights a week.
- Shut off the phone at dinner.
- Plan one weekend event per month with family without the phone.

Objective: Start a blog.

Key Results:
- Create a blog website in two weeks.
- Schedule time in the calendar to write blog posts every other week.
- Post and share blog posts on social media every month.

As you can see, OKRs are more specific, simplified, and measurable steps. As with the other frameworks, the key is to make the goal exciting and obtainable. Another example of detailing what success and goal achievement would be like is below.

Goals + Success Spectrum

This template was shared with me by Dr. Joey Page, Austin Public Schools Superintendent. While I have used it more specifically for professional goals, there is a great opportunity for application in your personal life as well. The Goals + Success Spectrum is a toolkit designed to help you get clear about goals and outcomes. It defines success along a spectrum—from minimum to target to epic—which gives you a much more nuanced and specific sense of what you're trying to accomplish as well as different scenarios for success and failure (Wu n.d.).

The template is free and accessible on their website: https://fasterthan20 .com/toolkit/goals-success-spectrum/ and looks similar to the visual below:

Goals + Success Spectrum.

Failure	Minimum	Target	Epic

This is a different way to not only set specific goals but visualize what they will look like when you accomplish them. Let's look at the previous goals within this framework.

Goal: *By the end of the quarter, I will have a weekly routine set to eat healthier by planning out meals every week and drinking more water and less soda during the workday.*

Failure	Minimum	Target	Epic
I will continue my pattern of unhealthy eating and face physical and emotional consequences.	I will start weekly meal planning and see our food budget decrease (less eating out). By substituting water for soda, I will see my energy become more balanced throughout the day.	We will have better eating habits (more vegetables, fewer carbs) and see a positive financial impact to planning our meals ahead of time.	Our family will adopt a more consistent habit of eating more fruits, vegetables, and lean protein over carbs and fast food. This lifestyle change could increase our chances of exercising more often and maybe challenge us to enter a family 5K run/walk!

Goal: *By the end of the week, I will set up regular batching and mega-batching sessions for paperwork and email tasks during my workday so I can leave work at work and be more present at home with my family.*

Failure	Minimum	Target	Epic
I continue down the pattern of working 24/7 and feeling frustrated and unfulfilled.	I will start utilizing inbox zero (emptying my email inbox) three days a week in which I only will check my emails at specific times and follow the 3 D method (delegate, delete, do something with it) to cleaning out the inbox. By limiting my time grazing on email, I can be more present for others and in classrooms more often.	By batching scheduled tasks (email, evaluations, reports, newsletters), I can have more concentrated time on those tasks and do them with better fidelity while also creating margin for classroom visits, and deep work on bigger projects.	I will leave work consistently at 4:30 without guilt and absent of taking piles of work home!

So, with these resources, what is stopping you from focusing on specific goals that align with your dreams? And how can this impact the calling to the work you wish to do and life you want to lead?

Focus in, Focus on: Getting Goals Right

Strategic goal attainment takes the development of a thoughtful plan with intentional checkpoints ensuring what you set out to do will get done.

- **Habit Checkers.** Let's say you have a goal of being more active in the day. Using your technology for good (not evil, or hours on Facebook) can help. Using an app that counts your steps, a playlist that gets you moving, or setting up a ring challenge with your 17-year-old can help encourage participation and a little competition.

- **Ask a friend for help.** Schedule out a 5K with a friend. Knowing someone else is counting on you helps make you accountable. Years ago, I had a goal to increase the number of books I read in a year. In talking with others, I found out I wasn't the only one, so we started a monthly book club. This afforded me accountability with my goal and gave me time with friends and a chance to read books I wouldn't always pick up for myself.

- **Make a plan.** The process of writing something down helps put clarity and accountability in play. For example, if you wanted to run that 5K in two months, mapping out your weekly miles and runs will ensure that even if you miss one or two, you will still be ready for the race. A reading goal requires you to set time aside at night, or on the weekends, to read. Completing a project at work requires you to map out chunks of time without multitasking to get it done.

- **Celebrate big and small successes.** Seriously, you have to write it down, schedule it out, and celebrate it when you are done. Right now, I am tracking how many words I have written in this coffee shop in Ft. Smith, Arkansas. When I hit the magic 36,000-word mark, there is a lavender-honey latte waiting for me at the counter.

Pick one thing and do it well

Or saying it another way: the deep work of goal achievement. Cal Newport offers a goal-setting strategy meant to reduce the complexity of a task, and, like Nemo, find ways to keep swimming even through the rough seas of social media.

In *Deep Work*, Newport shares a strategy that has helped him focus on the most important work and set boundaries around distractions (Newport 2016, pp. 194–196). First, he identifies a few goals in his professional and personal life. When developing the goal, keep in mind to limit the list to what is most important in the achievement of these goals. Next, list two or three activities that will help you achieve the goal (specific enough that you can picture yourself doing them). Finally, he asks you to consider the tech tools you utilize and determine if the tool has a substantially positive impact, substantially negative impact, or little impact on your participation in the activity. After this, you will have the hard choice of continuing to do things that are not serving you in the goal achievement or surrendering your cell phone (or Pinterest account) to become more successful with your goal attainment.

GENTLE REMINDER: GOALS CAN BE DONE SANS PERFECTION

1. **Give yourself grace.** Will your first attempt at a SMARTER goal leave out one of the "r"s? Possibly? Will you set your sights on achieving your goal five days a week and only hit the mark for three of them? Probably? Grant yourself some forgiveness during the start of this work and build on small steps toward growth, goal attainment, and habit stacking.

2. **Phone a friend.** A better way to achieve goals is to bring someone on board with you. If you are looking for accountability to leave school earlier, ask a coworker to walk you out. How about staying off your phone during family time? Ask your spouse or a demanding 17-year-old to take it from you. Recruiting others will help you stay accountable to yourself and those around you.

Doing the Homework: Going Deep, Not Wide with Goal Achievement

What goals are you setting this quarter?

- **Personal:**
- **Professional:**

What do you need to do to achieve these goals (no tech, low tech, and tech included)?

- **Personal:**
- **Professional:**

What activities (or technology) need to go away so you can achieve these goals?

- **Personal:**
- **Professional:**

CHAPTER 7

Restarting: How to Push Past Paralysis

Are you living life,
Or is your life living you?

#PrincipalinBalance

I can do anything for about 10 days. No wine? No problem. Run two miles for 10 days, even in unpredictable Minnesota May weather? I am your person. Even setting a goal to plan and prepare family meals for two weeks in a row is a stretch, but I have gotten it done.

But when week three creeps up on me, I start to get . . . fatigued. A social event calls for "just one glass," a headache in the morning and evening activities push the two-mile run to . . . well, none. And by week three my family has returned to grabbing dinner at the Kwik Trip three blocks away.

Pa · ral · y · sis \ pər-'ra-lə-səs: a state of powerlessness or incapacity to act

At times, setting goals can be the easy part; it is achieving them that can be the struggle. There have been times when I have set a goal (like writing 4,000 words for this book in a weekend) and it seems that every curveball and roadblock is headed my way (in this example, it came in the form of 90 days of free Apple TV). That kind of setback can send me into a shame spiral of disappointment and disillusionment and becomes a bigger setback toward the outcome.

PREVENTING GOAL PARALYSIS

There are a few simple questions you can ask as you wrestle with goal paralysis and determine your next steps.

1. **What is your goal?** If you can't remember the goal you are working on right now, it might not be that motivating, or meaningful, for you. Or you might have too many goals you are trying to achieve at one time. Try focusing on no more than four goals at a time. If you are using the Balance Like a Pirate framework (Johnson et al. 2018), you might want to focus on three out of the four quadrants. Otherwise,

challenge yourself to set a goal for work and one for life to focus on them for six to eight weeks.

2. **How does it fit within the goal framework?** If you use the SMART or SMARTER framework, is the goal exciting? Specific? Time-bound? If it is lacking a few of these initials, you might be losing steam before you start.

3. **When are you set to achieve the goal?** For example, if you initially set a goal to run a marathon, but the race isn't for 16 months, it might be too far ahead to get motivated now. Instead of setting multiple training plans, try cross-training, yoga, or another activity to keep you active, healthy, and ready for race training a few months from now.

VISUALIZATION = ACTUALIZATION

Go deep with detail. The more time you spend thinking about what you are thinking about, the better the opportunity to catch any derailers or detractors from what you are trying to do.

For example, if you want to go back to school for a degree, the more you think about the details, the better clarity you have around what has to get done, and how much time it might take to do it. Going back to school isn't as easy as just showing up on campus and walking into class. Steps include finding a college, looking at requirements, comparing costs, choosing courses, mode of classes, reviewing degrees and timelines. If you don't think deeply about these steps, you might miss something like a deadline, a school you didn't know about, a cohort model that is running in a city close by, or a chance to complete most of the classes at home and online. By visualizing what you want, you can get clear on how you want to achieve it.

Give it a try, take one of the goals you created, and run it through this visualization activity.

1. What would success look like in achieving this goal?
2. What steps would I need to take to finish?
3. What would be markers of mini successes along the way?

4. What are possible barriers to completing this goal? And how can I prevent them from occurring?

5. How will I celebrate completing this goal successfully?

REFLECT, REVIEW, REVISE, AND REPEAT

I am an over-analyzer, if that is even a word. A former assistant principal used to call me on it all the time. I would overthink a field trip, an assembly, a staff meeting, a presentation, to death. I would obsess about the details and have back-up plans from A to N ready to go in case we needed them.

If I was the over-analyzer, he was the "just do it and figure out how to fix it later" leader. So as a team, we worked really well together as a balance of too much, not enough, but just right.

It is important to reflect on your goals regularly. If you want to fully achieve something, it will take time to revisit the steps in case something comes up that might compromise your timeline. Questions that I have used in the past include:

• What did I set out to accomplish?
• Did I achieve it?
• If yes, how will I build on this success?
• If no, what went well, what didn't, and what would I do differently next time?

Guided questions for this type of process can be found and developed in multiple ways. The key in making sure they work is to find the right rhythm for you.

ROUTINE + TIME = CONSISTENCY

This reflective process is best implemented when it is a consistent part of a routine you already have set. For me, goal reflection occurs at the end of the week. I look at what I set to accomplish at the start of the week, and on Friday afternoons I take 20 minutes to review what I accomplished, what I didn't, what worked, and what could be improved.

If you are working on a collaborative goal at work, this routine could be part of a regular meeting. For example, a monthly review of your site plan with site leadership offers structure, accountability, and time to adjust if things aren't moving forward according to the plan you set out to accomplish.

Often the overthinker in me will sit and spin on a framework or set of questions for months, whereas my work partner would jump in and adjust as the months went on. While neither approach is always right, timing and consistency is key. Before starting a goal, set up accountability checks in your calendar, and put them on agendas for meetings. By setting the structure before you start, you are more likely to reflect, review, and revise something before it is too late to change or fix.

HABIT STACKING

When you are moving toward a goal culture at work and life, sometimes you can hit roadblocks that might derail all of the work. One the best wats to push past a sense of powerlessness is to build on the wins from other goals you have achieved or are working toward achieving. This process is called habit stacking: building on the success of a habit by adding one new thing you want to start doing.

James Clear speaks to the importance of habit stacking (Clear 2018) in his book *Atomic Habits*. Taking that a step further, you can build upon previous goal success by adding on to one goal that has turned into a habit to build on your capacity, confidence, and clear understanding of what it takes to turn a goal into a habit.

Let's try this method with a few personal goals. Imagine these are a few of the goals you would like to achieve at home over the next year:

- By October I would like to have a routine at home in which I am not checking email or working after 5 p.m.
- By December I will have a system in place for meal planning for our family, so we eat in better and eat out less.
- In the New Year. I would like to allocate more time for my hobbies (writing/reading) at home.
- By May I will use my Peloton bike five times a week (cycle, strength, yoga, outdoor run/walk classes).

If you apply the stacking method to goal achievement, you might see the pattern that is seamless and does not seem like another thing you have to do. Follow along:

- Once you have accomplished the goal of not checking email after 5 p.m., you have created a margin in your calendar at night to focus on meal planning (December goal).
- After a few weeks of building the meal-planning schedule and ensuring other members of your family can help, you could schedule two nights a week where someone else takes over meal planning/prep so you can build back time for your hobbies.
- Now you are six months in, you can't remember a time where you worked every night and find the break refreshing, making you more productive at work the next day. Meal planning is a habit your whole family helps with, and you now have less guilt and more excitement about taking a night or two off from meal plan/prep. You have joined a book club or are consistently posting on your blog. To continue building on the healthy lifestyle, you now end (or start) your day with a 20-minute Peloton class and track with the app to celebrate your success!

Make sense? It does take some time on the front end to find the connections on the goals you want to achieve and how they can work together toward success, but once you figure it out, it works. If you go out too soon with a plan to achieve all your initial goals, you are going to find out quickly you don't have the bandwidth to adjust to the change in such a short amount of time.

WHEN DOING TOO MUCH IS TOO MUCH

Have you ever pulled into the parking lot and not remembered exactly how you got there? Or how about watching a movie while on your phone, and not remembering much of the plot or characters? Have you had a conversation with someone, and they clearly knew you were not present in the moment and missed an opportunity to sustain or enhance an important relationship? There is such a myth to the importance of multitasking and trying to get it all done, and that myth has repercussions that will impact your work, life, and the relationships you are attempting to build between both.

multitasking \ 'məl-tē-,ta-skiŋ: the performance of multiple tasks at one time

Early in adulthood I thought multitasking was a sign of prestige. I mean, if you were so busy you had to do multiple things at one time, you had to be important, right? In our focus to be it all for everyone, we found out that when you try to do it all (or a few things at one time), nothing really gets done, or worse yet, you can't remember what you were doing!

In *Switch on Your Brain*, Caroline Leaf speaks to the concept of milkshake-multitasking as something that decreases our attention, making us less able to focus on our thoughts and habits (Leaf 2015, p. 94). She states that every rapid, incomplete, and poor-quality shift of thought is like making a milkshake with your brain cells and neurochemicals. This makes the myth of multitasking more of a reality of inconsistent and unreliable results in anything you are trying to accomplish. The only thing multitasking is proven to deliver is more mistakes and mishaps in whatever things we were trying to accomplish.

I have plenty of instances of milkshake-multitasking in work and life, but one stands out. My youngest son, Isaiah, is a diver. Diving is a sport I thought was injury free until I watched him come so close to the board, I now make sure there is a defibrillator in every pool he dives at! If you watch diving, you know that you wait, and wait, and wait until your diver is up. He gets on the board and from start to finish it is about a 25-second event, and then you wait . . . again for the next dive. Early on, I made the mistake that I could multitask during the wait. I brought my computer and would answer emails in between dives, and someone's email would turn into Amazon shopping, which would lead me to a quick scroll of my social media feeds (work purposes only, of course). Inevitably, I would miss one of his dives due to my inability to stay focused being present. My heart breaks at the fact he probably got up on the board, looked up, and saw me glued to my computer or phone instead of watching his incredible accomplishments in the pool.

In this example, I not only share the dangers of multitasking but also my kryptonite: the cell phone.

I am a proud digital "Gen Xer," meaning I picked up the use of cell phones, smart phones, laptops, and email starting in my twenties. This lack of learning in my tweens and teens means I made up for lost time as an adult. I was dysregulated, unfocused, and preoccupied with technology more so than I want to admit. I was really into technology. And most times I was sucked into doing one thing and looked up hours later realizing I was lost in something completely different. And to be honest, I might have forgotten what I was looking for in the first place.

Just because
technology *is on 24/7,*
doesn't mean you have to
be on it as well.

#PrincipalinBalance

My cell phone takes up more real estate in my day than I would like to admit, and sometimes more than I really think it does. How often do we just turn on the computer at home to check one email, and look up and realize we are late getting dinner ready, or lost track of time and are now late to pick up a child from an evening practice? If you have ever gotten sucked into something on your phone or computer, and lost your focus or purpose at home, you are not alone. When we have competing priorities, no one wins. You are either going to respond to that email in a hurry without context or with frustration. Or you are going to miss that dive, or conversation with your teen, or a split-second chance to connect with your spouse. Staying focused on one thing and doing it well isn't just nice, it is necessary as we move forward into being more balanced, less busy, and with more abundance in our actions.

Back to the Isaiah diving story and how I have flipped the script on multitasking and removed my phone from the equation. I now take a new approach to watching his events. I take my phone but keep it on airplane mode. That way I can record all his dives for him to review afterward, without fear of seeing a notification, a text, or tweet pulling me away from the priority of being a diver's mom.

Take it from me and what I learned the hard way. Multitasking doesn't work. The more often we can single-task, we support the parts of the brain that help us with deep focus. This deep focus helps us accomplish something with deeper complexity and increased fidelity.

PIVOTING WHEN SOMETHING GOES WRONG

But what happens when . . .

- You get injured when training for a marathon.
- You are transferred to a new job mid-year after planning long-term goals in your current setting.
- Something significant happens in your personal life that impacts your professional life.

piv · ot \ 'pi-vət: an adjustment or modification made (as to a product, service, or strategy) in order to adapt or improve

Be careful not to quit when something happens that shifts the goals you had set. The opportunity to reflect, review, and revise is essential in seeing how far you have come. This also allows you space to adjust the goal that still gets you to the end you visualized.

Often, the goals I set look different at the end than the start.

- It may start as a goal to complete a marathon with a personal record. I end up adjusting to finishing a marathon and enjoying the day with a friend.
- Setting out to adopt a child adapted to supporting former students in times of need and serving a purpose that looked different than I had predicted.
- Staying a middle school principal at Ellis made a major revision to lead future and former students as we developed an online school within our district.

So, I get it. On a personal and professional level, the best laid plans can develop holes or be completely shelved without notice.

Good leaders make plans and set goals.
Great leaders ground themselves in purpose.
They are prepared to pivot and adjust to
achieve excellence in the end.

#PrincipalinBalance

ENSURE YOU ARE OFF TO THE RIGHT RACE

This reinforces what we have already stated: the goal you are setting needs to be grounded in purpose. Doing something because you see others doing it is rarely a solid reason to take it as a personal goal. If it is something you are excited about doing, you will do anything in your power to get it done.

Before you start something, make sure you really, really want to finish it. Having a purpose and plan in mind for a goal ensures you will fight to find a way to finish it . . . even when it gets hard.

THRIVING THROUGH THE MESSY MIDDLE

Leading in middle school feels like a daily Groundhog Day of the messy middle. Middle school students understand something one day and completely forget it the next. I watch teachers explain appropriate hallway behavior, homework practices, and routines within the class, and inevitably I watch a student, later, ask to clarify or do the exact opposite of what we had just practiced.

Sometimes I feel like my hand is permanently glued to my forehead as a symbol of the face-plant reaction I have after hearing another "They did what?!?!" story.

The messy middle isn't just reserved for tweens and teens, but for setting goals and getting to the finish line. The messy middle is an opportunity to forget why we started or stray back to old habits because the finish is too far away. This is where things like "it's only one donut," or "just a quick run through the drive-thru" happen, or "I will get back on track with my exercise next week."

Know in advance that you are going to have hiccups and detours on this journey. The point isn't to do it perfectly, the practice is to get it done.

FINISHING STRONG

Here it is, you can see the final stretch! The race is up ahead, the data review is on the calendar, or the event you have been waiting for is finally here. Finishing strong requires a disciplined approach all the way through. The last thing you want to do when accomplishing something is be too exhausted, frustrated, or distracted to really enjoy what you achieved.

Stay rested. I know it sounds weird, but when you are most exhausted and just want to push through, it is really a good time to pause. Finishing something strong means you are mentally and physically prepared for the end. I could never understand the taper for my son's swim season, until I saw dramatic improvements on his splits and time at State Competition.

When training for marathons, the weeks leading up to the race have the least number of miles. Why? So you can be physically ready for the big race ahead. Take that practice off the road and into your professional goals, leading up to a major accomplishment. How can you slow down and make sure you are ready for the final push to the finish?

Maybe it is making sure the weekend before a big week is mainly offline and with family so you can feel rested and ready for the final few days before the end of the quarter or a bigger presentation. It could be taking time away from rehearsing a meeting to go to a movie or play with your kids. While it seems counterintuitive to slow down before the end when instead you could speed up and finish, there is a key perspective you would miss: enjoying the final leg of the journey.

My favorite part of marathons is the final mile. It always comes up quickly and I always feel like it goes too fast. Seeing all the spectators cheering you on, the music, the pictures, and just that final moment. What I rarely tell people is . . . I had probably walked more in the previous 5 miles than I did in the other 21.2! That's right, I slowed down my last 5 miles so I could really enjoy the final one. It seemed so counterintuitive, but looking back I wouldn't have wanted to race through that last mile sore, hurt, or sick and miss the time to enjoy the accomplishment.

So, in thinking ahead to the goal you want to achieve, how can you plan to slow down at the end to finish strong?

Once you set on the few goals you are going to work on for a season in life, the next step is setting systems in place to ensure you are prioritizing the right work and letting go of the rest.

FINDING A GROOVE AND GIVING YOURSELF A PASS

I hope you are seeing the theme: less perfection and more purpose. Pushing past perfection will be the key to decreasing the paralysis you feel when trying to implement new goals and habits in your life.

This is just a pause in the book to restate the importance of forward progress, just do a . . . single . . . thing. And celebrate it.

Reframing to Find a Groove	
You set out to do a 30-minute run and only made it 10 minutes? What happened?!?	You got out and completed a 10-minute run! Way to go!
You wanted to leave work at 4:30 every day, and this week, with conferences and a school concert, you left work three days late.	This week I had an opportunity and poured into my school community. Next week I will shift back to leaving work at 4:30.

Reframing negative self-talk into a growth-minded opportunity to learn and change will help accomplish the goal when the curveballs of life are thrown at you.

GENTLE REMINDERS: GIVE YOURSELF GRACE DAYS

One of my strengths that can also be a vice is my ability to be disciplined. If I say I am going to do something, I will do it, even if it comes at a cost. One example of this was when I was training to complete a half-marathon with a friend. I had one of those weeks, a sick dog, sick kid, and late nights at work that significantly impacted my sleep. Instead of taking a day off on the running plan to sleep in and catch up, I pushed through. I got up early and ran an awful training run, and then I got sick. Lesson learned: listen to my body and stop focusing on the task list.

Grace days are chances to move away from legalistic practices around meeting your goals.

These can take the form of a "grace meal," when you are trying to eat out less but have a scheduled book club dinner with friends. Or you could have a "grace Saturday" where you run into work for three hours to complete work for the week ahead, knowing this proactivity will help you manage the busy evening family commitments ahead. Or if something terrible happens at home or school and you need a "grace week" to regroup after a tragic loss, an unexpected hurt happens, or a shift in your career path presents itself and you need time to just be by yourself to process and plan.

Being a *Principal in Balance* is not about achieving at 100%. *Principals in Balance* give themselves the grace they freely give to those around them. And by modeling taking breaks from the habits and goals you are setting shows others it is okay to do the same.

Doing the Homework: Five Ways to Sustain Goal Growth

Okay, you have the tools and strategies to start, as well as ideas when roadblocks come your way. Now it is your turn to put this into action. Take time to complete the following steps and for extra points post to Facebook, Instagram, or Twitter and tag me (@JessicaCabeen) with #PrincipalinBalance Good luck and get going!

1. Write it down (pick a framework—SMART, SMARTER, etc.).
2. Make a plan (what do you have to manage in order to lead?).
3. Tell others (share your goal ideas with others for motivation, accountability, and encouragement).
4. Prioritize (stop throwing darts). Align priorities in your life with the time in your day.
5. Celebrate! Create opportunities to celebrate the big and small successes.

PART **III**

LIVE COLORFULLY

WHY LIVE COLORFULLY?

We have been running an unsustainable race. Trying to do it all, for everyone, all the time is not a long-term plan for success in thriving at work and life. Feeling bad for slowing down, and shame for saying no, has to stop. Becoming resilient means looking for ways to live well while having a life.

Live \ 'liv: to maintain oneself

Colorfully \ 'kə-lər-f(ə-)lē: full of variety or interest

This requires us to color outside of the imposed lines on the life plans. The lines that say we have to work 50 hours a week, or to do things well, we have to post everything and show our accomplishments in a polished, filtered way. The lines that shame and guilt us if we color even just a little bit outside of them. To focus on living a life we want to lead, we have to let go of unhealthy practices and the shame cycle that surrounds the expectation to do it all. Being everything for everyone isn't worth losing our lives over.

If you are struggling with a deep level of sadness and, more specifically, guilt over something, self-care might mean journaling, reflecting, or having a conversation with a trusted friend or therapist. But if you are experiencing a deep level of sadness due to feeling lonely or isolated, spending time with family, friends, or, for me, my pandemic puppy, might be the better way to utilize self-care to work through your feelings.

HOW CAN YOU TAKE CREATIVE CONTROL?

Living Colorfully requires you to do one thing . . . lead your life. Often we get caught up in the pressures of popular opinion. We pass up the things we really enjoy or wish to do because others want us to do something else. As someone who has a wall of degrees and many detours toward her current profession, I wish I would have learned this lesson earlier. Do what you love to do, and stop worrying about what others will think.

cre · a · tive | \ krē-'ā-tiv: marked by the ability or power to create.

con · trol | \ kən-'trōl: to have power over

I like to think our life journeys line up like the old Frogger videogame. When Atari consoles came out, I loved playing Frogger. The goal of the game was to guide the frogs back to their home, navigating past busy streets and a river full of logs and other hazards.

What I learned after hours upon hours of playing that game parallels what I have learned in life:

Sometimes in order to go forward,
you have to take a step back,
pause, or go sideways.

#PrincipalinBalance

Here are a few examples of taking the Atari game into action in my work and life:

- I left a promising career as a music therapist to pursue a teaching degree.
- I left a school I loved teaching at to take an internship at the district level.
- I left a community I had invested in for seven years to move to a city that was closer to family.
- We adopted from a country that had many connections in our new home for our son to continue to have meaningful interactions with his birth culture, while learning to navigate life in a new world.
- I left a school I loved to spend a year learning how to be a principal and a parent in the same year and same school. Six years later I did the same thing again, hopping a log that brought me back to middle school while my eldest son was an eighth grader.
- I started writing years before I ever received a book contract because I enjoy telling stories and helping others.

- I worked with community and state partners speaking and developing content and curriculum well before I ever was paid for it, and I still volunteer my time to projects that serve a deeper purpose.

I lead in all areas of life more unconventional than most, but in the end, I love what I am doing and can see how the side steps, hops backwards, and the pauses in the game have helped the outcome in the end. All of this to say, none of it was easy.

- Going back to school required me to spend time studying on the weekends.
- Leaving the classroom meant I lost the daily connections to the students I loved.
- Moving away from Saint Paul to Austin, Minnesota, had a greater culture shock and adjustment than I ever expected.
- International adoption requires consistent reflection and intentional planning to ensure I was outside of my comfort zone to provide experiences and opportunities for Isaiah to experience his culture as often as we could.
- While principaling and parenting in the same school can be awesome, it can be awful as the boundaries between those roles are deeply blurred.
- Writing is a very vulnerable and humbling experience, regardless if 2 or 2,000 people read your words.
- Speaking and consulting takes you away from your day job and family, which means when you come back you are behind, and the balance of both those demands can be daunting.

But with the pros and cons listed on my biggest hops in my personal and professional career, I can look back and say I directed every move. Every hop, slide, or jump was my choice. Was it easy? Rarely. Did others think I was crazy at times? Of course!

CREATIVE CONTROL COMPONENTS: BODY–MIND–MOUTH

Taking creative control of your life requires you to know who you are, what you want to do, and where you want to go, while understanding that life may ask you to recalibrate, reset, or rest during the journey. The examples above span over 20 years of my life. And sometimes the most painful points felt like years in the pit, when looking back it was only weeks or months. And in reflection, the lowest points of the journey have taught me the biggest lessons and given me more insights that I could use moving forward than if the detour had not happened.

But what if creative control is a new concept for you? What if you have been following a roadmap written by someone else or for someone you thought you wanted to be, but have decided it is no longer what you want to achieve?

Taking creative control requires three key components Body–Mind–Mouth:

1. What goes into caring for your body?
2. What consumes your mind and time?
3. What comes out of your mouth?

It's time to take a deep dive into these three components and find ways for you to take back control and start playing the game the way you want to play it.

The next chapters will focus on two foundational concepts that support resilience in practice: self-care and soul-care. Self-care focuses on our health-care and all that encompasses. These topics include physical, emotional, financial, and spiritual well-being.

In Chapter 9, we look at self-care and how it can impact our purpose, health, and happiness, Chapter 10 defines the term soul-care and how pairing self-care and soul-care together build our resilience to tackle what is to come in a way that energizes us.

This next section challenges what we have been taught, and what we have imposed on ourselves regarding leading well *and* having a life. Be ready to feel uncomfortable and create a new picture for the life you want to lead. Be ready to adjust to making it fit who you are, rather than fitting into the picture you think everything thinks you should be.

CHAPTER 8

Finding Balance

What do you have to *manage* in order to *lead?*

#PrincipalinBalance

Overwhelmed yet? Rethinking how we have been living all these years can be met with regret, anxiety, and a sense of worry about how to really make this new life work. If you weren't worried at this point, I would be worried for you! Stepping away from the hustle and hurry and moving from fine to flourishing is going to take intentional work, reflection, and restarts.

You *can't be well* for others until you *prioritize wellness* for yourself.

#PrincipalinBalance

Throughout this work, you will fall off the schedule, forget to prioritize your well-being, and struggle to sustain some of these practices sometimes. When this happens remember these two words: rest and reset.

When we desire to have better self- and soul-care, it is essential to focus on your body, mind, and mouth. And you can't do that running from activity to activity, working 12 to 14 hours a day, 6 to 7 days a week, without a break.

SLOW AND STEADY

True to the Aesop fable, slow and steady wins the race. Slowing down not only means winning in the end but enjoying the journey. This is only accomplished when you focus on slowing down and seeking rest.

Rest \ 'rest: freedom from activity or labor

This part of the journey to becoming a *Principal in Balance* has been the most challenging. Slowing down and resting is not in my nature. I thrive on being on the go, wearing my busyness like a badge, and, unfortunately, tying my purpose too closely to my pace. This way of living has little quality to it, only quantifiable exhaustion.

John Mark Comer calls the outcome of this pace "sunset fatigue." By day's end you have nothing left to give to your spouse, children, or loved ones. They get the grouchy, curt, overtired you, and it's not pretty (Comer 2019, p. 49). Been there, done that, and ready to stop.

Seeking rest isn't as hard as you think, but you have to find ways to do it authentically that are tailored for you. If going for a walk sans cell phone stresses you out, or your seasonal allergies will wreck you for the rest of your day, then don't go for the walk. But if sitting in the backyard watching the sun come up or go down for 5 to 10 minutes brings you joy and peace to your day, then please add that into your resilience reservoir.

QUALITY, NOT QUANTITY

In the introduction to Alex Soojun-Kim Pang's book *Rest*, Arianna Huffington states the why so well. She shares that it isn't just about taking time to rest but being intentional about the activity and quality of rest. Psychologists find that people who don't keep busy during their free time, who don't check their email at night and on weekends, and who truly leave work behind when they go on vacation are happier, more productive, and more resilient at work (Pang 2016, p. xviiii).

When you treat rest like a check on your daily to-do list, you will complete it out of obligation, not out of relief or the opportunity to build resilience.

PERMISSION TO REST

Take a time out, or if possible, some time off. Recalibrate your sleep and get more of it if needed. Pull back from a lot of extracurriculars and extra committee meetings and pare down to the basics: sleep, eat, exercise, work, rest, repeat. To regain the strength and stamina to combat the stress and surging we all experience, it is important to find time to slow down and regulate.

re · set |\ (ˌ)rē-ˈset: to set again or anew

A hard reset. Have you ever had to do one on your computer? It is frozen, not functioning optimally, or something is just not right. Resetting your computer gives it a chance to fix any bugs or errors that might be slowing down performance and aid functioning properly. My question is, if a reset is good for technology, why not try it for ourselves?

"Almost everything will work again if you unplug it for a few minutes, including you."
Anne Lamott (*12 Truths I Learned from Life and Writing* 2017)

Just like when our computer or phone freezes up, a hard reset is required for yourself. Turning everything off, resting, and then slowly reacclimating back into our lives ensures we have the right portions, sizes, and things on our plate. Intrigued? Ready to try a reset for yourself? Focus on the following three steps: find the flow, break the script, and just keep going.

FIND THE FLOW

Building routines to ensure a reset is important, especially at the start of the process. Shifting your routines from a focus on others to an intention of taking care of yourself will be hard. This shift will take time and practice, and for a while you might feel guilty about this shift in priorities—but I challenge you to take it as a shift in perspective.

We have already talked about fine and flourishing and now it is time to add a layer to the process. Do you want to end your day with *fine*? Or do you want to start adding a little *flourish* in your reflection? Now, we are still going to have days, weeks, or seasons when getting it done is the best we can do, but that can't be the norm anymore. If we want to really enjoy the life we are living, we have to make intentional plans to live it and live it well. Flourishing in our day isn't about finishing "fine" but finishing with success.

After work, "fine" would be dragging in take out, and zoning out in front of the TV. However, "flourishing" could be walking in the door after work with the energy to spend quality time with family.

Fine is smiles and surface-level talk you won't remember a week later. Flourishing at work looks like engaging with others without looking at your phone, being able to remember specific comments or unique stories from others during that time, and being able to recall them later on, thus building a deeper and more meaningful relationship with those you serve within your schools/organizations.

Fine is like running out, worried more about getting back and getting to the next thing, than wondering what would be further down the road you always turn right on. Flourishing and self-care looks like going for a run, not just to get it done, but to really enjoy the time away from your phone, your other commitments or demands, and to memorize the views and feelings from it.

Once you start experiencing more flourish in your day than fine, you will feel it. Something will be different about how you end and start your day. A change in other's interactions and actions with you, and, ultimately (and most importantly), a deeper sense of joy and satisfaction in the work and life you are leading.

So, this sounds good, right? But how does someone go about changing the check-it-off attitude and start to integrate a check-in position for daily routines, activities, and interactions?

BREAK THE SCRIPT

In Chip and Dan Heath's book *The Power of Moments*, they share the secret sauce to breaking the script (Heath and Heath 2017, p. 72). A script is a general routine, process, or activity you do every day. This could be anything from how you answer the phone at work to how you show up for family events. Breaking the script is making a strategic surprise in the routine or ritual. For driven, type-A, control freaks, we are already sweating on this one. But we should be.

Too often we go through
the *motions* of our life and
we miss out on *moments*.

#PrincipalinBalance

I hurry and hustle through the day feeling good about checking off all the boxes, but upon reflection, I can't remember much of the details of my interactions and actions with others. I just remember I got "it" done. I can reflect on interactions I had with others that left a pit in my stomach. Someone was reaching out for connection, and I responded cooler than normal because of all the things in my mind I thought I needed to get done. I missed an opportunity to really connect with someone. Epic Fail on repeat more than I want to admit. And when I am not in the flow of flourishing, I continue to rinse and repeat the surface level failures at I rate I don't want to admit to moving forward.

This isn't about feeling ashamed for moving too fast at the pace we have been thinking we need to be running at. However, it is going to give you a compelling reason for the change. Running through your life means you are going to miss most of it.

Let's look at some examples of how we can break the script.

Morning Routines

I keep bringing up the concept of a morning routine because how we start a day shows how we live our lives. If you get up and race out the door, you continue to perpetuate a life of hurry, hustle, busy as a badge of honor (or a weight of regret), and an "I'm fine" attitude, not one of flourishing.

So, let's break down a morning and see how to break a script.

7:00 a.m.   Up, after hitting snooze four times.

7:10 a.m.   Let the dog out, wake up kids, get ready for work.

7:30 a.m.   Tell kids to shut off the TV as they haven't gotten ready yet, realize you didn't flip laundry last night so what you wanted to wear isn't ready, and, oh, the towels in the dryer have been there for two days.

7:50 a.m.   Found something to wear, kids in the car (after yelling at them . . . twice) and race to work "almost" on time.

Breaking the script has a few rules. Before you break it, you have to first understand it.

So what story are you telling with your morning routine? And are your actions matching the routine?

If I could visualize the example above, it would include some running between bedrooms, laundry rooms, and chasing down kids (and pets). I could see the anger and frustration bubbling up (but not out—yet) from the reminders and hiccups in the steps to get out the door. Frustration, feelings of failure and exhaustion, and the day just started. Not the story I want to write every day, and not the one I want for you either.

So now that you understand what story you are telling (whether you like it or not), you can find ways to break it.

What feelings do you want to have as you walk out the door? What experiences do you want your kids to remember about their mornings with you when they are adults? I only ask because the morning routine above was mine for the first six to seven years of my oldest son's life. I wonder what he remembers of this time as I would most likely like to forget how my hustle and hurry impacted how he started his day at daycare and school. And while I can't go back in time and change how I did things, I was able to break the script and provide a little variety in the morning experiences moving forward.

A few staples that changed so the general script had more flow and flourish and less fine and frustrated in action included:

- Getting up an hour earlier so I could complete my own Miracle Morning.
- No TV or electronics for anyone until we were ready to leave (it is amazing how much better toddlers, tweens, and teens listen when you aren't competing with cartoons and social media feeds).
- Outfits ready the night before, bags packed and at the door.

Now for the fun by adding in the spontaneous breaks in the script:

- Occasional runs to the coffee shop for hot chocolate/latte.
- "Donut bribes" if we are ready on time (which in my spouse's terms is early) where we swing through a local donut shop en route to church or other special activity.
- A ride to school versus riding on the bus.
- A longer walk with the dog (now that makes him super happy and me as well).

While these are examples that work for my family, I realize they might not be for yours. Donuts might not fill your bucket or enhance an experience for your family. But how has the experience for all changed from Example A to Example B? Which set of circumstances sets everyone up for success versus stress?

Try your own example here:

My routine now	What I want the routine to be

What can I flip to change the experience and move from fine to flourishing?

JUST KEEP GOING

Finding the flow and flourishing is the foundation. Learning how to handle the hiccups by shifting your mindset and refocusing your time on self- and soul-care is essential, so you don't stop when you fall off track. I tend to have a mental picture of Dory from *Finding Nemo* (Unkrich and Stanton 2003) saying "just keep swimming" when I find my focus on self- and soul-care is off. But if you need a little more support than a blue tang in your head, here are a few more ideas.

Gratitude journaling. While what got you here might not get you to the next destination, reflecting on what has worked builds your confidence and capacity to endure hardships and hiccups. I have included this in my morning routine; I use it throughout the day as an intervention if I sense I am spinning or spiraling a bit away from my self- and soul-care practices.

Try this now: set a timer for five minutes and free write anything and everything you are grateful for, down to the things you take for granted (having a place to sleep, something to eat), and things you are hopeful for (student success, career promotion). By intentionally focusing on what is going well for five minutes, you can shift your mindset from negative to neutral. . . and then eventually back to positive.

Reframe situations or circumstances. My superpower is reframing. I used to be an amazing "awfulizer," until I realized that focusing on what wasn't working . . . wasn't working for my general demeanor or mindset. I think working as the principal of the "Happiest Place in Southeastern Minnesota," aka the Woodson Kindergarten Center, for six years helped shift my frame. Yes, I was the leader of a building of 400 five-year-olds. It was a mix of sunshine, bubbles, laughter, and grace every day. When kids made mistakes, we found ways to forgive quickly and move on. When you surround yourself with happiness and joy, it is hard not to have that spill over into other aspects of your life and future positions.

When I became the principal of Ellis Middle School after the kindergarten center, it was a culture shock, to say the least. I give the analogy of moving from sunshine and bubbles to vaping and Tik Tok. Middle school gets a bad rap, and it has a few challenges to overcome. When I entered the position, I came with a mantra that guided my years of leadership in the building, my actions and interactions with others, and how I hoped others saw me when I showed up in spaces:

EXPECT THE BEST

Before analyzing, awfulizing, or demonizing an interaction, experience, or mishap I step back and use this mantra to guide the next thing out of my mouth. For the first six months on the job, I am sure people thought I was crazy. In reflection, people have said they were waiting for the "kindergarten in me" to leave. But I worked really hard to see the good in everyone, especially before having a hard conversation. Much of this came with practice and daily self- and soul-care checks, but I attribute this attitude to my ability to reframe. In the world of middle school, this mantra was a daily guidepost. When a student made a comment that seemed out of context, I assumed a positive intent. Instead of walking away or making assumptions, I asked questions to find out why the response was short or negative. By staying regulated, I was ready for whatever bathroom hijinks, snap chat snafu, or social media meltdown was happening.

Here is your homework: look back on today and find a specific action or interaction that didn't go well. How can you reframe your thinking on this event from what went wrong to what went right?

In my gratitude journal, I focus on identifying three things that went well the day prior and three things I am looking forward to that day. What might surprise you (again, back to breaking the script) is I try to choose at least one thing I am *not* looking forward to and find a way to reframe it.

- Having a hard conversation with someone turns into an opportunity to build better communication skills and deeper relationships.

- An evening informational session on another upcoming soccer season or graduation meeting is a chance to spend time with my growing boys before they become adults.

- Covering a classroom due to lack of subs becomes a way to build relationships with students, support staff, and show families a leader can lead from the office or a language arts classroom.

Give it a try. What is something you are not looking forward to doing today? How can you break the script and find a way to learn from it, enjoy it, or become better for it?

Measuring the gain, not the gap, isn't easy. We are wired to focus on what went wrong, instead of looking deeper at what went well, or what we learned in the process. Slowing down and practicing some of these techniques to help you right the ship and stay on course will prove beneficial in work, life, and the relationships with others you want to enhance and maintain.

GENTLE REMINDER: MEASURING THE GAIN, NOT THE GAP, ISN'T EASY

We are wired to focus on what didn't go well and too often we miss what went right. If you didn't quite hit your goal, what did you learn in the process?

Doing the Homework: A Weekly Detox

Sometimes the best thing to do when you are stuck is nothing at all.

A day of rest, a day of no work, and time to reflect and be grateful for what you have.

If you are ready to have a hard reset and a day to unplug, try these steps:

Ground rules:

1. Set a time frame: 10, 12, or 24 hours.
2. Create expectations from menus below.
3. Set an out-of-office or notify those closest to you for account-ability support.
4. Implement!

Sunday Principal Playlist:

Choose from this menu of activities to remove from your 10-, 12-, or 24-hour detox.

- No email.
- No schoolwork.
- No social media (be specific: Instagram, Twitter, Facebook, Other _____).
- No reading of schoolbooks, journals, blogs, or other resources.
- No work texts.
- Turn off all phone notifications.
- Put your phone away for the day.

Choose from this menu of activities to add to your 10-, 12-, or 24-hour detox.

- Go for a walk.
- Watch a movie without multitasking.
- Read a book for fun.
- Clean, organize for fun.
- Garden, plant, grow something.
- Get back into a hobby: _____
- Spend time with friends.
- Date day or night.

CHAPTER 9

Redesigning Self-Care

Self-care is not selfish,
and at times it can be life saving.

#PrincipalinBalance

This is the chapter that might make some of us uncomfortable. Putting ourselves first has never been in the cards. Social media pressures us to compete with others and in our professional lives. Too often we have been taught that nonstop hustle and hard work is the only way to be successful.

This view is unhealthy and can lead us down a path of unhappiness, burnout, and blow-ups with those we love and care about. When you have been at your worst at work, you have probably not been the best to yourself either. Racing out the door in the morning and running late might make any course correction later in the day seem like a disaster instead of a small detour.

One of my many wake-up calls in the quest for sustainable self-care practices came a few years ago—the school year with the never-ending snow days.

In Minnesota it is normal to have a few snow days every year. But not 11 . . . in two months. It almost felt like we were out of school more than we were in it. I think it was literally months before we had a full week of school, and we all felt it. Lost without my regular routine, I noticed I had an appointment for a mammogram the following week. And even though we were all home on snow days, I felt guilty about taking a day off when we were all finally in school, so I postponed the appointment once, then twice, and finally went after the school year ended.

Two mammograms, an ultrasound, and four biopsies taught me a lesson I needed to learn: self-care is not selfish and at times it can be lifesaving. Prioritizing our health and our lives isn't diminishing others, it is developing the bandwidth and boundaries to be able to live a life and lead it as well.

Self-care \ ˌself-ˈker: care for oneself

In Dr. Adam Saenz's book *The Power of a Teacher*, he speaks of educator well-being as a way of breaking the decompensation cycle, which is the failure in the coping systems we keep in place to make our lives function. When we decompensate, we start to lack the capacity to do what we know we should do. As we continue to decompensate, we become less effective and more anxious. This leads to a loss of seeing our calling in this work, and a worry of treating our career as a paycheck instead of powerful calling. (Saenz 2012, pp. 19–20)

Self-care has a direct correlation to our callings in work and in life. When you digest the significance self-care has on your physical well-being, your emotional regulation, and the impact on resilience and calling in your life, it is hard to stop ignoring this essential part of our lives.

Let's look at decompensation from a personal perspective. I usually run at least 8 to 10 miles a week. I started to miss regular warm-up and cool-down stretches and started to skip meals and increase wine consumption at night. While out for a run in the late fall, I felt something pop and a pain set in that required me to stop. I tried for another block to hop/jog and realized it wasn't working. Instead of calling for help, I limped back to the house. Instead of icing and looking for pain relievers, I continued with my day. While most would think a trip to the doctor or physical therapist might help, I just wrapped up my knee with tape and tried to "walk through it."

My days now started without running, and instead of the runner's high I had for years, I felt lower than ever before. As frustration set in, I tried to push through it, hopping through a half-mile run/walk with the dog. I took the stairs with both feet on a step because range of motion wouldn't allow for all my weight to be on the "bad leg." Most meetings at school we held with an ice pack and elevated leg. Driving was difficult and getting in and out of the car was a full-time job. After five weeks, sadness set in, and shortness toward others became the norm. Historically positive and optimistic, I became short and cynical; others noticed. Finally, a dear friend sat down and told me the truth: your injury has caused you to become a different person, one you don't even see you are becoming because of your bitterness of your situation and your inability to see that you really need to ask for help to push forward.

I learned, in a very hard and prolonged painful situation, something we all need to remember. Self-care is not selfish and at times it can be lifesaving. I lost my primary self-care strategy with that injury, and instead of seeking help and realizing how running elevated my physical, emotional, and mental well-being, I stuffed my feelings down and became more frustrated with my circumstances, struggling to see that I needed help. Others around me saw the change but didn't immediately see the connection that self-care has on our overall health. Luckily, someone close (and brave) was willing to speak up and share their concerns for my health and well-being. They also helped me find the health that would get me back to a place of loving what I did, even when one of the things I loved to do needed to be adapted during this time of healing and recovery.

Four months later I laced up my shoes and dusted off the running leash for my pandemic puppy and set out for a long run: 1.5 miles. Prior to the injury I would have been embarrassed to say that was as far as I went, but now I realized that running the miles wasn't the why of the work. Running was my chance to have quiet time during days of constant noise. Those four months without this in my daily routine impacted not just my physical health but my occupational calling.

It doesn't take a knee injury to decompensate. It could be a change in job positions, a loss at work, or a death close to home. Whatever the situation, without self-care strategies, we lose the ability to cope with disruptions in our day that can derail us for weeks, months, or completely out of a career.

If that isn't a compelling why for self-care, I don't know what is.

PUTTING OUR BEST SELF(-CARE) FORWARD

So what? Now what? How can we start prioritizing self-care and stop pushing it aside?

To show up as our best selves for others,
we have to prioritize taking care of ourselves.

#PrincipalinBalance

What is self-care? It is way more than a bubble bath, or a walk outside. Self-care are practices that support our whole selves and give us space in our day to develop who we are outside of our occupational titles.

The National Institute of Mental Health (2021) defines self-care as taking the time to do things that help you live well and improve both your physical health and mental health. When it comes to your mental health, self-care can help you manage stress, lower your risk of illness, and increase your energy.

The biggest turn-off to self-care is in the title. For self-care to work, you have to do something for yourself. That doesn't mean signing up for a 5K when you hate running or reading for fun when that is the furthest thing from fun you can imagine. The importance of establishing regular self-care routines is to do something you enjoy. Then you will see the positive effects on self-care in your physical and mental health, not a frustration or part of the day you loathe, but one you look forward to.

BUILDING YOUR SELF-CARE PLAYLIST

So far, we have focused in on why self-care is important, and now it is time to move from theory to practice. What are the categories of self-care and how can you find ideas and activities that will help cultivate resilience and long-term healthy habits?

During the pandemic, my dear friend and academic mentor Dr. Lana Peterson introduced me to the power of playlists for students in school. The purpose of a playlist is to provide students with sequences of activities that upon completion will help them with mastery of a skill. In our school, we started to incorporate playlists into professional development. Teachers would tackle activities on the playlist in an order that made sense to them and could do so at their own pace, in their own classrooms, and demonstrate understanding in many ways.

So, what is a self-care playlist? It is practical activities broken down into specific categories. To provide variety, we have grouped self-care practices into six different categories. You can research other types of categories that might be tailored more for your needs, but these six are a great start.

- **Emotional:** habits that help release emotional stress.
- **Practical:** ways to reduce stress by creating systems at work and in life.
- **Physical:** activities to improve daily living and regular checkups.
- **Mental:** engaging in activities that keep your mind focused.
- **Social:** taking intentional time to spend with family and friends.
- **Spiritual:** finding ways to recalibrate our calling and purpose in life on a regular basis.

As the leader of your own learning, you can choose from different activities that fit your mood, your needs, or what will help you thrive rather than just survive.

Here are a few examples:

Physical	Emotional	Mental	Social	Practical	Spiritual
Walking	Writing in a journal	Reading a book	Activities with friends	Organizing email	Spending time in nature
Sleeping regularly		Playing a game	Spending time with spouse or significant other	Decluttering spaces	Worshiping
Staying hydrated	Creating (art, jewelry, etc.)	Going to a museum		Prepping/ planning meals	Journaling/ devotionals
Eating well					
Getting medical checkups	Playing music		Calling a family member regularly	Planning wardrobe	

Take some time to identify three or four categories and four or five activities you would enjoy doing and would help you regulate yourself. These activities should help you gain the skills to navigate the challenges that come up throughout the day.

By regularly engaging in self-care, you will start to feel better in the six categories. You will also find the time in your mind and space in your day to achieve the goals you set in the previous chapter and complete them with energy left for the rest of your life.

PUTTING SELF-CARE ON YOUR CALENDAR

Okay, so how do you start? Calendaring your life is essential to ensure you prioritize your time in the right order. To be comprehensive in this work I do both my personal and professional work together on the same calendar, especially if the two worlds uniquely intersect (evening work commitments, family commitments during the school day).

Another point of frustration in establishing sustainable self-care routines is the element of time. Most people will say they don't have time in the day to do something for themselves. I challenge you to reframe that to prioritize yourself before setting the rest of your schedule.

First, brainstorm everything you have to do, not what you think you have to do (committees, volunteering, additional meetings). Sometimes I think of it as the things only I can do. For example, at work, I am the only one who can sign off on the bills, complete the teacher evaluations, develop the vision for the school, and implement the professional development for our school. I am not the only one who can supervise lunch, monitor hallways, attend all the concerts and special events outside of school, and be outside for morning and afternoon bus duty every day.

If it helps, after you complete the brain dump, start sorting into categories:

Personal	
Only I can	**I can have others help**
Take care of my health	Meal planning/prep
Bible study	Laundry
Exercise	Household chores
	Shuttling to practice
	Walk the dog

Now think about what you want to do, if you only had time to do it and add into the brain dump:

Personal	
Only I can	**I can have others help**
Read more for fun	Meal planning/prep
Sign up for a 10K	Laundry
Budget for an upcoming date weekend	Household chores
Finish writing this book	Shuttling to practice
Take care of my health	Walk the dog
Bible study	
Exercise	

When focusing on the new additions to the columns, utilize these questions to start thinking about scheduling:

- When are the most optimal times for me to get this work done (i.e., right away in the morning, midday, or at night)?
- What needs to go away for me to have intentional time to complete these new self-care supports?
- What resources do I need to be successful?

Here is an example in practice for starting a regular workout routine: I want to exercise for 30 minutes five days a week.

- When are the most optimal times for me to get this work done (i.e., right away in the morning, midday, or at night)? *My schedule can be more unpredictable after work, so getting up and exercising right away in the morning will best help me accomplish this goal.*
- What needs to go away for me to have intentional time to complete these new self-care supports? *Getting up 20 minutes earlier and not checking email and social media before I exercise will allow me the time needed to get moving in the morning. Having my kids' clothes and bags ready to go the night before means our morning routines will be easier. I can have my husband wake up the kids while I am working out and before he goes to work.*
- What resources do I need to be successful? *Exercise clothes, a training plan, bookmarking Peloton courses, signing up for morning classes at the YMCA, and a goal sheet I can check off each day of exercise to show progress.*

CREATIVE CONTROL OF SELF-CARE

What goals do you have for your personal health? If you don't have any, you should. Health is not just about losing weight, drinking water, and exercising. It can be about targeting increased energy, being more mindful, resting, or searching for space in your day to connect with friends or family. There are so many ways we can see that self-care can be lifesaving. So, what is it for you? What is something you want to do but never seem to have time to get it done?

Taking creative control for yourself requires you to take control of your schedule, habits, and any established routines or practices that won't serve your new purpose. These shifts don't happen overnight and require a level of intentionality we historically reserve for work and professional pursuits, not our own health and wellness.

Going back to that ideal week, let's say one of your creative control objectives is to decrease the amount of processed sugar in your diet. What if you set aside time on Sundays to plan meals and shop for the week? Knowing your goal is to decrease processed sugars, you could proactively spend 60 to 90 minutes finding recipes and mapping out a healthier grocery list instead of running through the store on the fly and grabbing things off the shelf that might be easy but not healthy. What if you committed to using a calendar on the refrigerator and posted the upcoming meals for the week so if you are running late one night, someone else can get it started? Better yet, look ahead and see if you can delegate a few nights to someone else if your evening commitments might tempt you to just run through a fast-food drive-through instead of having someone put something in the oven? Creative control requires a level of commitment and foresight to see potential curves in the road.

Don't make excuses, make adjustments.
Alex Toussaint (2022)

#PrincipalinBalance

We put off for ourselves the things we are eager to support in others. How many events, games, races, fundraisers, or other activities have you gone to for someone else, but not done for yourself? I used to take my own children to music lessons weekly, but then didn't give myself time to play piano or practice drums regularly at home. Or all the times I sat in the parking lot of a venue waiting for practice to end when I could have used those 15 minutes to go for a walk around the block with the dog.

If we spent the amount of time we use making excuses to adjust our routines, we might be a little more successful in achieving our self-care goals and establishing manageable habits.

The best way to make room for yourself is to schedule time for yourself. Create an ideal week or create a document that has every day of the week and time increments from 5:00 a.m. to 8 p.m. on it. Before you schedule work, family, or other commitments, put yourself on the schedule first. When you make an appointment with yourself, you are less likely to ignore it or forget about it.

GENTLE REMINDER: MAKE SURE YOU ARE PLUGGING INTO THE RIGHT OUTLET

As you are working on creating self-care playlists and routines, make sure the activities you include fit into the categories of need.

Doing the Homework: Creating Your Own Playlist

What self-care practices will you need to start, stop, or continue to support your growth in becoming a *Principal in Balance* while also helping you achieve the goals you have set? Use the template below to identify what areas and aspects you will focus on in the next three or four weeks.

Physical	Emotional	Mental

Social	Practical	Spiritual

CHAPTER 10

Restorative Soul-Care

Find your worth
outside of your work.

#PrincipalinBalance

Have you ever done something for yourself? Something you didn't think you really had time for, or needed to do? But that something when done, made you feel really good?

For me, that is my role as an occasional drummer at our church on Sunday mornings. My purpose for taking this on was to find a way to serve in our church. My husband is a master at greeting others and thrives on Wednesday nights with his high school youth group. I, on the other hand, have become introverted on the weekend to regain bandwidth for my day job on Monday, and the youth get enough of me during the week.

I played drums in college and I have a drum set to practice on at home. But why in the world would I take on another responsibility when I already have enough to do with my day job?

Soul \ 'sōl: a person's total self

Soul-care is starting to grow roots in our daily lives. It can have spiritual implications and application in overall well-being and health. And while self-care looks at emotional and physical health, soul-care is an opportunity to enhance focus on your mental health and build the capacity to seek calm over the chaos our lives currently run in every day.

In Chapter 1, we talked about resilience being our core, our nucleus. Soul-care is a protective layer reminding us that taking care of ourselves is important, not selfish or shameful. Soul-care prioritizes thoughts, feelings, and capabilities that when tended to, allow you to thrive in any circumstance. While self-care creates habits to lead healthier lives, soul-care creates healthy thought patterns to build upon our resilience in life and at work.

Soul-care involves the thoughts and feelings that come from prioritizing your emotional, physical, and mental well-being. Intentionally utilizing self-care and soul-care together helps you to prioritize these activities in your life.

132

So back to becoming a Sunday drummer. While it is not something I have to do, it is something I enjoy doing. Playing music is fulfilling for me, it brings me joy, and it fits my more introverted weekend personality. This break from my regular routine refills and refuels me for the week.

Taking on a habit that feeds my soul offers perspective. I can't worry about that email I received Friday while trying to transition between songs and beats on the drum. I am certainly not thinking about the week ahead when I am serving my church in this way. And I love playing the music I listen to in the car during the week and using the lyrics to guide my mantra for the day and circumstances ahead.

Someone once challenged me in regard to my focus on self-care and soul-care and how I could prioritize time in these areas over working on site plans, staffing changes, and academic successes for our students. My response was something I wished I could have articulated years ago: to lead well, you have to live well and that requires you to find things that are fulfilling your life. If you don't take the time to refuel your soul, you won't have the passion and drive necessary to move your school forward and build on a positive culture and academic success.

While self-care helps you to manage your well-being, soul-care helps you to really figure out what you are feeling and how to improve your well-being.

#PrincipalinBalance

To be honest, the awards I have received for my professional accomplishments came from prioritizing my personal life first. Stepping away on your days off provides you the bandwidth and boundaries to stop overthinking work and start refueling and feeling good about yourself. So, when you return to work you are refreshed and ready to engage in your calling.

Soul-care. This is our heart-care. It is how to have more of what makes our heart happy, and how to protect our heart from things that can break it. As a dear friend put it, soul-care is the intersection of your identities. It is helping us understand that who we are doesn't directly equate to just what we do. And when we are right with our souls, we lead better with our body, mind, and what comes out of our mouth.

SOULFUL PRACTICES AT PLAY

What are soul-care practices? And how can I integrate them into my day? For an initial onboarding to this area of practice, let's look again at the six areas of self-care.

- **Emotional:** habits that help release emotional stress.
- **Practical:** reducing stress by creating systems at work and in life.
- **Physical:** improving daily living and regular checkups.
- **Mental:** engaging in activities that keep your mind focused.
- **Social:** taking intentional time to spend with family and friends.
- **Spiritual:** finding ways to recalibrate our calling and purpose in life on a regular basis.

If the above list is related to self-care and the development of reasonable, achievable, and sustainable habits for our work and lives, what would these areas look like as hobbies?

- **Emotional:** activities that help us regulate our responses to stressful situations.
- **Practical:** routines that recalibrate our mind and mouth when agitated.
- **Physical:** breaks in our day to provide space to respond and rethink situations, not just react.
- **Mental:** hobbies that help calibrate our calling in work and life.
- **Social:** going deeper than coffee—asking for help from trusted friends, coworkers, or even a therapist when things get dark.
- **Spiritual:** finding ways to serve or spread out our calling in deeper, more meaningful ways.

As the leader of your own learning, you often may find that some of the activities you utilize in self-care also might find a season of support in the soul-care domain. Here are some ways you can build hobbies to help create healthy thought patterns and enhance soul-care practices in your day.

Physical	Emotional	Mental	Social	Practical	Spiritual
Finding a hobby such as swimming, running, cycling, or taking classes for physical fitness.	Starting a blog. Journaling, reflecting, and reframing circumstance.	Learning new coping techniques for stress. Finding hobbies outside of work.	Joining a book club. Starting a Bible study or other small group.	Setting boundaries between work and life. Utilizing a planner to keep organized and track the implementation of these hobbies and habits.	Serving others by volunteering. Supporting your calling by finding ways to cultivate it outside of your title or position.

PRUNING WEEDS: TAKING CREATIVE CONTROL OF YOUR MIND AND TIME

I can't keep a plant alive to save my life. Gardening would not be on my playlist for self-care or soul-care. It doesn't provide me joy, but I am using this example of pruning anyway.

A few years ago, I found out about succulents. They are really hard to kill. Succulents became my new favorite word when I spent a year trying to be an indoor gardener. At one point, I had four plants I kept alive for three months! But I had a hanging plant that was barely hanging on. The leaves and branches were overgrown, and were turning yellow instead of the greens and purples I was supposed to see (according to my gardening app). The app encouraged me to pull over 70% of those leaves out. I kept refreshing the app and I finally looked on websites, as well, because I didn't believe pulling out so many of the branches would make it healthier!

Weed \ 'wēd: an obnoxious growth, thing, or person

We all have weeds in our lives. Things that take up time in our day and space in our mind that negatively impacts our quality of life. Think about someone or something that might be driving you crazy right now. A tweet from a troll, a negative email, or a coworker whose behaviors are bringing you down. How often are you thinking about this situation, circumstance, or person? Is it impacting other areas of your life? Does worrying or feeling guilt or shame about it impact how you are interacting with others? If yes, you have a weed and it is time to uproot it.

Upon deeper observation, I noticed the stems of that hanging plant were really just dead or not connected to the foundation. It looked full, but it was unhealthy. In our lives, we are recognized and praised for doing it all, but in reality, we are doing too much. When we are running at this insane pace without breaks, it will lead to burnout. That full life we thought we wanted is really overgrown and in need of some significant pruning.

When it was time to remove the weeds from that plant, my husband showed me how to prune it back, and while initially I was disappointed that it shrunk significantly, once it was hanging again it looked so much better.

Too often we think bigger and bigger is better. Having a full plate is more fulfilling than paring back and focusing on a few things. Pruning can be really, really hard. But eventually you get back to healthy soil and a firm foundation.

What is taking up time in your day
and space in your mind?

#PrincipalinBalance

THE PROCESS OF PRUNING

So what activities feed your soul? What would you enjoy doing more of, if you just had the time? Figuring out what you want to do first, helps you prune out the things in your way.

In my example of Sunday drumming, to be ready to play, I needed to block out time to be fully present for practice and performance. That means Sunday is a no-work day. No meetings, no activities, nothing to rush to so my mind stays focused on the service, not what I need to do next. Occasionally, I have had to run to Thursday practice from one of my boys' sporting events or to get back to a middle school concert. In those moments, I am not fully present in rehearsal, and I am not enjoying the soul-care practice as much as when I have extended buffers in time between the code-switching roles of principal–parent and person.

And while there are multiple aspects to pruning, time is important, but so is focus when you are in the moment. So how can you stay focused on soul-care and weed out the other thoughts in your mind?

PUTTING SOULFUL PRACTICE IN PLACE

This one is hard for me. I tend to get stuck in my head and spin on things more than necessary. I can read into body language, interactions, or something online for hours. It consumes my mind and time and leaves me defeated and discouraged.

If I am brave enough to address the elephant in my mind with another person, I often see that what I thought was insurmountable is just a chance for me to be vulnerable. I can see it for what it really is, and it's not as big as I thought it was.

So, how do you stop spinning and start seeing through the weeds of negative thoughts and unproductive reflections of interactions?

1. **Get off your phone.** Often our spiral starts from something we saw on social media. Our phones can be a barrier from letting go of the shame cycle and negative bias around situations and circumstances. That may mean keeping your phone off until work starts, setting timers for use on certain social media streams, or snoozing, unfriending, or unfollowing people. Whatever you need to do to take control of how you use your phone, do it.

2. **See the good.** When you are stuck and frustrated, stop and pay someone else a compliment. There is a very strategic reason I wait until the end of the week to complete my Positive Office Referrals (PORs). PORs are chances for me to recognize the great things going on within our school by our students. All staff can nominate students for things big and small, then Ms. Sarah calls students down to meet with me. We talk about the reason for the nomination, how they feel about being acknowledged for the good they are doing, we take a picture,

and I send it home with a personal note from me as the principal. This 30-minute habit can totally turn around a day. For me, Fridays are historically the hardest day of the week. I am more tired than I was at the start of the week, problems and complaints have piled up. By taking this intentional time of gratitude, I change the trajectory of the rest of the day, and it helps to end the week on a more positive note.

3. **Ask a friend.** This one might be hard, but it is helpful. If I am stuck rehashing a negative situation in my mind, I will ask a trusted friend to help me unpack my feelings and assumptions around the situation to see if it is as big when spoken aloud as it was in my head.

My dear friend and work thought-partner Chris has a guided mantra for me when he sees I am struggling to let something go. He tells me to be like Elsa. If you haven't paid much attention to the famous song from the movie *Frozen,* here are the lyrics that have helped put challenging things into perspective, situations or circumstances I have had a hard time letting go:

Let it go, let it go
Can't hold it back anymore
Let it go, let it go
Turn away and slam the door
I don't care what they're going to say
Let the storm rage on
The cold never bothered me anyway
. . .
funny how some distance makes everything seem small
And the fears that once controlled me can't get to me at all (Buck and Lee 2013)

Having a friend who is willing to point out the things you can't (or don't want to) see is a helpful strategy in pushing past the thoughts in your head and moving forward. Brené Brown utilizes her square squad to get this approach into action. Get a 1-inch-by-1-inch piece of paper and write down the names of people whose opinions really matter to you (Brown 2018, p. 22). This is your square squad.

So, when life seems insurmountable, reach out to someone who is close to you and willing to help you talk out what is troubling you to gain insight, advice, and support.

4. **Get out of your head and get outside.** This doesn't necessarily mean a nature walk, but taking a walk or walking away from the space you are in currently can change your mindset and perspective. If I am getting the "inner agitated" feeling, you know the one where everything feels uncomfortable, awkward, or frustrating, I get up and go for a walk, visit a classroom, or spend time with my family or our dog. Getting out of your head might require you to get away from the current environment to gain perspective or pause the thoughts that are spinning.

   I have a personal flaw. I am sometimes late or juuuuust on time to meetings. While this is a flaw most times, sometimes it is a coping strategy. For example, I may just have had a very hard conversation with a student and parent about a choice made in school that will have significant repercussions. I might have had to hear about an unfortunate circumstance in a staff member's life that will affect their focus at work. Or I have had to deliver news about a denied promotion or a termination. Leaving those meetings and trying to enter another without a pause to process means I take the emotions from the previous meeting into the next one. This can cause the unresolved processing to leak out in things I don't mean to say, or body language that comes across the wrong way. So instead of taking the fastest route to the next meeting, or before the next meeting comes into my office, I take the long route. I might get a drink of water or make tea, or, after the really challenging meetings, I try to connect with kids—even if just for a few seconds—before I head to the next meeting. Taking a quick turn off to recalibrate gives you the opportunity to process what happened before you go on to the next thing and prevents you from taking an additional emotional baggage along the way.

5. **Get a Do-Done, Done.** When I am frustrated, irritated, or agitated about something I am working out in my head, I pause and do something else. Finding ways to help you course correct and get going again can also help you put the thoughts in your mind in perspective. While writing this book, I was struggling to get the inspiration to start my goal of 5,000 words for the weekend. One hour in and only 698 words. I was frustrated. My negative self-talk was spinning a narrative that wasn't helping me see past the word count and the calling to write. However, before I could really boil over, I stopped. I got up and out of the office and went for the two-mile run I had scheduled

later for that day. While outside I was able to reset and found a new angle for a hook that got my word count mojo going again. There is a gentle reminder in this example:

Sometimes it is okay to pause instead of pushing through.

#PrincipalinBalance

At times, taking a break prevents a breakdown, the pause provides a moment to regain purpose, and the interruption a chance to recalibrate your intentions.

Asking for a friend . . . when you are stuck, what helps you course correct and get going again?

With all the focus on your mind, how does that correlate to the time in your day? While it isn't an exact ratio mantra for me, in course correction "what you think about is what you think about," and that is what gets accomplished. When you are supposed to be focused on one task (like reading this book), but you are attempting to multitask by watching a movie at the same time, your thoughts are divided, which means either you will have to reread this chapter, or rewatch part of the movie.

Being intentional with your time is a significant investment, one in which if you don't pay attention to it, you will pay consequences. Think about your morning routine and try a time audit. From the moment you get up to the time you get in your car to head to work, what are you doing? Here is one of my time audits:

- Making coffee: 5 minutes
- Checking email: 30 minutes
- Scrolling on social media: 20 minutes
- Exercise: 20 minutes
- Journal/devotional time: 10 minutes
- Breakfast: 5 minutes
- Total time: 90 minutes

Yikes. I've been up for 90 minutes before I have to get ready for work, but what did I really get done? In this example, more time was spent on social media and email than on soul- and self-care combined.

The way you start the day sets the tone. So, what does this example say about the priorities and purpose of the established morning routine that has been established? Creating a morning routine that prioritizes soul- and self-care puts you back in creative control of your time, which will directly impact your mind and the next step—what comes out of your mouth.

CREATIVE CONTROL OF YOUR MOUTH

There is a process between body, mind, and mouth. If you don't take care of the first two, you will figure it out when it comes out of your mouth and by then, you can't take it back.

When you are tired, frustrated, overwhelmed, and running on empty . . . how do you have the capacity to have meaningful and intentional conversations?

In my book *Lead with Grace*, I share an epic example of this. I was exhausted, frustrated, and questioning my calling on a regular basis. A text came through from someone and I immediately lost it. I sent a text to another friend venting my frustrations, except I accidentally sent it to the person I was frustrated with. Epic, epic fail.

This can happen in small ways as well. You have a frustrating day at work, and you come home to a sink full of dishes and dirty towels all over the house. Is your first response one of grace and support? Or fueled with the frustrations of the day, you blow up on your family?

In an article from social worker and therapist Hope Arnold (2018), she describes emotional leakage as what happens when a person's self-control has failed, and their inner feelings are revealed and expressed more intensely than preferred.

In my middle school girl vernacular, I have coined this as a really, really bad hair day. When things seem to not be going well, stuffing your feelings won't work, and you will usually know that it isn't working when it is too late. It is important to find outlets to release the fear, failures, and faults of the day before it affects those you love and care about.

If you struggle with this aspect of balance, or if you find yourself needing a few new strategies, here are four ways to prevent the emotional leakage impacting your long-term relationships with others.

1. **Step away.** If things are ruminating in your head and your thoughts are spinning, set a timer for five minutes and walk away. If you were mid-sentence into something, write the last thing down and then leave it. Just the process of seeing something different can help you to see the situation in a different way.

   This strategy is key when transitioning between two environments like work and home. Let's say you are pulling into the garage after a long day with looming projects for tomorrow. In the example of the dishes not being done, if you don't take intentional space between the two environments it will impact both negatively.

   Before I leave work, I have set habits to ensure I leave work at work. That might be answering the last emails for the day, writing down what needs to get done tomorrow, or setting time to work through some of the challenges that happened during the day. If you work from home, you can still set those boundaries. Maybe it means turning off apps that will alert you to work tasks during the evening, or you might shut the door to your home office when you are off the clock.

   On the hard days, give yourself a buffer of quiet time to collect your thoughts and transition to the next phase of your day. You will be less likely to leak out on others the stress from the previous environment.

2. **Write it down.** What is really bothering you? Sometimes what is on the surface is masking the deep feelings, doubt, or the real dilemma. By journaling in the moment, it provides your brain an opportunity to really dig deep and see the foundation of frustration.

   I highly suggest you write down your thoughts of what is bothering you on paper so you can throw it away when done, especially if you name people in part of your frustration. The last thing you want to do when trying to stop the leak is have someone accidentally find your frustrated words after the fact. And please, please, please do not do this exercise on any type of electronic platform. At the moment, you might feel better sending off the email, commenting on the post, or shooting out the text, but I know from experience it will only hurt you and others on the receiving end.

If this is something that needs to be addressed, write down your concerns and review it with someone in your square squad, a supervisor, or trusted colleague. They might be able to offer you strategies, support, or suggestions on ways in which your concerns can be heard and not hurtful.

3. **Take a deep breath.** This helps, especially if you are working on responding to challenging electronic communication. Sit up tall and take three deep breaths. When we are stressed, we tend to constrict our bodies, and forget to breathe. When you see the subject line or name on an email that tends to cause you stress, what do you do? Chances are you clench your jaw, stop breathing, and start making assumptions about what is written before you even open it.

Try it right now. Sit up as tall as you can, look up (not down at your computer), and take three deep breaths. The process of stretching out and expanding your own body helps recalibrate your inner organs, which can help your emotions and give you a physical break.

4. **Shut it off.** When you attempt to be on for everyone all the time, you will find that your bandwidth for sending and receiving information is negatively impacted. By taking a break from technology and things that bring you back to work or stressful situations, you are never really shutting it off. Taking regular detoxes from technology (email, social media, TV) provides boundaries and bandwidth to stop doing things that numb your responses and start doing the things that feed your growth.

GENTLE REMINDER: DON'T LET YOUR WORRIES OVERTAKE YOUR WORTH

The more you incorporate soul-care practices, the less you see negative and unhealthy thought patterns creep into your life.

Doing the Homework: Pruning Your Practices

What soul-care practices can you start, stop, or continue to support your work in becoming a *Principal in Balance* while working toward the goal you set at the start of this work?

Use the template below to identify what areas and aspects you will focus on in the next three to four weeks.

Physical	Emotional	Mental

Social	Practical	Spiritual

PART IV

LEAD BOLDLY

Taking Charge by Building Bandwidth and Setting Boundaries

We are almost to the end of this journey. Early on, we started with the compelling reasons for seeking balance and finding ways to lead at work and have a life. We learned the importance of resiliency, the dangers of languishing, and how to identify surge capacity.

Next, we focused on our purpose, how to set goals, and identified ways to battle barriers, burnout, and breakdowns to make sure our intended goals stay clear. We came out of that section with renewed purpose, and a plan we can implement, review, revise, and celebrate progress along the way.

Living Colorfully offered ways to look at self- and soul-care in practical and tangible ways. Learning to lean into these two areas is fundamental in becoming a *Principal in Balance*. It will help us avoid old habits that lead to burnout, and the old "busyness as a badge" routine we are breaking away from.

To lead at work and in life in a new and intentional way, it is time to put all this together. Strategically, this is the last section because it will be the hardest. Saying no to others and yes to ourselves is the hardest shift many of us have to make. Too often we sacrifice our needs so we can take care of others. What I wished I had learned long ago, I share again with you now: recognize that the best you can give to others starts by taking care of yourself first.

When we *live well*, we *lead well*.

#PrincipalinBalance

This section is built upon the ground rules of building bandwidth and setting boundaries. To start that process, you look for guideposts and guardrails in work and life. These will be the signs that help you stay on the new path, the one where you prioritize your own well-being before others. The guardrails help you from slipping back to being on all the time and feeling frustrated and exhausted when you get home at night.

Bandwidth might be a newer concept for some. It is the emotional or mental capacity to do something (or really anything). I think we have all seen our bandwidth blow up. Therefore, we must recognize the signs and put

146

things in place to stay within our bandwidth. And this is where boundaries come into place.

Boundaries are knowing when to say no, and by saying no to others you are saying yes to yourself. Boundaries are needed in many aspects of work and life, and recalibrating your bandwidth is a great place to start. The examples in these chapters will help you find ways to understand why you should say no, and how to do it well.

Breaking patterns of conforming to old practices and peer pressures takes dedication that is not easily acquired. But I promise the work moving forward is worth it.

CHAPTER 11

Stopping the Sprint

When you say *yes to everything,*
you do *nothing well.*

Have you ever hit a wall? A time in your life where things feel overwhelming and taking the next step forward seems impossible? When my walls come, they show up in different ways. Agitation, frustration, and a sense of "just get it done" are common feelings when I am frozen, stuck, or exhausted. And the impacts are evident across my work and personal life. In my quest to just get it done, I usually do it poorly.

If I just hurry up and send the report, I inevitably forget a section, a key person to send it to, or it is so bad I must send multiple revisions.

At home, when I hit the wall, I usually just zone out, binge TV, or can't make the simplest decision (like what to eat for dinner).

In pursuit of well-being, hitting the wall leaves me too tired to tackle self-care activities such as exercise, journaling, or healthy eating.

You can be a leader who makes bad decisions or
good ones.
But don't be a leader who is *too exhausted* to make
a decision.

#PrincipalinBalance

In this mode, I am more concerned about just getting it done, and less worried about doing it well. So, when you are heading down this road, how can you find signs to help you stop and recalibrate to be a *Principal in Balance*?

guide · post | \ 'gīd-ˌpōst \: indication, sign

The end of the year and the start of the year for educators and leaders is a prime example of looking for the signs of burnout, blow-ups, or frustration that can leak into all aspects of life.

- **Increased frustration.** Ever have a moment that you go nuclear over . . . well, nothing? A normal request causes your head to spin and a whole different personality shows up and comes out of your mouth? When I am most tired and in need of recalibration, I tend to let my mouth work before my mind does. As a middle school principal, I see tweens and teens have major meltdowns over minor situations all the time. And during the start and end of the school year, I see it in educators, parents, and myself.

- **Lack of sleep.** This happens to me in significant seasons of stress. I will wake up in the middle of the night, or struggle to go to sleep with my mind racing about what has, might, or will happen. When things are really out of sync, I will even wake up on a Saturday, thinking it's a Thursday! A loss of sleep during stressful seasons will not help regulate your emotions, but instead make self-regulation even more of a struggle.

- **Decision fatigue.** Oh, this one. Friday hits me hard. I get home and can't decide what to make for dinner, what to do for the evening, or plan for the weekend. Decision fatigue can show up in the small things because you have had to make a lot of big decisions in your weeks.

- **Physical symptoms.** These are the easiest to see, but usually come later. When you are running at your surge capacity for too long, your body will show the wear and tear through many different symptoms. Stomach ailments, headaches, panic attacks, or getting sick due to stress are common for all of us. And then our unobtainable moral compass kicks in and we continue to push through while feeling less than our best. And you can guess what happens. The burnout builds and these triggers become guaranteed signs of stress overload.

So, what are your triggers? When do you know you are overwhelmed, stressed, or not your healthiest self? It could look like minor irritation, lack of focus, or difficulty making even small decisions. Learning what it looks like helps you to stop before it starts.

By focusing on healthy boundaries and developing a strong understanding of your bandwidth, you can utilize your guideposts to help you stop saying yes and start saying no.

GUIDEPOSTS AS CHECKS AND BALANCES

Another use of guideposts are ways of indicating danger ahead. Using caution when implementing new boundaries and bandwidth in your life is tough. Again, you are going against the popular grain of hurry, hustle, multitasking, and micromanaging every aspect of work and life. Instead, you are going to lean into less time online and learn from putting margin in your day, as well as mindfulness practices.

Guideposts can help keep your new lifestyle in check. When you are watching for the signs of overload, overstress, and overcapacity you can recalibrate quicker with fewer symptoms of burnout and blowups.

All of this is going to take time, practice, and intentional actions that will be different than what you have always done. And that means taking charge of your time and activities, and learning what needs to go.

- What are signs that you might be overcommitted at work?
- What are signs that you might be overcommitted at home?

Use these questions to find what is taking you off course from your goals and calling. Be brave and ask a friend to answer the questions for you. Sometimes it takes someone else to point out ways you are dysregulated so you can recalibrate sooner. Once you know the signs, then you can build the guardrails to protect yourself.

guard · rail | \ 'gärd-,rāl \: a railing guarding usually against danger

Middle school hallways. They are a memory we can't forget. Trying to get from one class to the next, stopping at your locker, connecting with friends, or spilling the tea, and then racing into the next class when the bell rings. As a middle school principal, I have tried many different strategies to help these adolescent brains and bodies get from first to second hour without injury, drama, or stress (for adults and scholars). But it is a middle school, there are 840 of them and only one of me, so things will go wrong occasionally.

One of those times was during state testing. We had changed our daily routine and put a two-hour testing window in the front end of the day and then shortened the rest of the classes. The theory was that the first part of the day was an optimal time to test. Doing it in large chunks allows students to focus and decreases hallway traffic. What we didn't predict or expect was the chaos that would ensue when the testing was over; we had students attempt to pass without the hall-passing bells.

Without the four little "ding, dings" spaced four minutes apart, kids and staff lost it! Teachers let kids out two minutes early, some lost track of what their next class was, and a few other kids just chatted in the main entry ways, oblivious to time. We thought it was a once-in-a-career moment, until it happened again the next day. Students couldn't regulate without the bells and the clocks that indicated how much time was left to get from class to class.

They lost their guardrails, and I nearly lost my mind.

You most likely will find out when you need guardrails when things go off the mark. There could be 840 middle schoolers standing in the hallway waiting like Pavlov's dog for the passing bell. Or it could be any one of the guideposts described above. The bad news is you won't know when you need guardrails until you are off the rails. The good news is if you put them in place, you only have to go off the rails once.

In that middle school example, because we had gone so far off the rails, we had to course correct quickly and with great prescription. I got on the intercom and announced every passing time. We split the grades so only one grade was in the halls at a time to bring the energy back down from "middle schoolers on Red Bull" to "regular middle school." The halls became calmer again, students and staff could get from A to B in under four minutes, and we were back on track. Going forward, we had a detailed plan for any days that would need this type of structure in the future.

Once you know when your guidepost is gone, you can start to establish guardrails to protect it. Often guideposts are broken due to overcommitments, which impacts your physical health. This could be having back-to-back meetings all day, or multiple evening commitments that interrupt your routines or sleep patterns.

BUILDING THE RAILS

If your guidepost is maintaining eight hours of sleep most nights of the week, what types of guardrails could you implement to protect this need? Planning your calendar ahead is one option. If you know you have a soccer game one night, and basketball practice the next, it might be easier to say no to supervising a band concert that would make three late nights in one week.

REGULAR MAINTENANCE

When you set the guardrails in advance, your elevator speech to say no is more automatic, more immediate, and more easily executed. Enforcing these guardrails makes execution easier as well. Back to the evening example. If asked to attend another evening event, a response could be "thank you so much for thinking of me, unfortunately I already have two evening commitments this week." The only way you know if the guardrails work is if you try them out. Do they help maintain or elevate the healthy balance you are seeking?

BOUNCING OFF

Just like the guardrails on the side of the road, sometimes you need to use them. Let's say you said yes to the third evening event of the week, and by the following afternoon you are beat. Instead of blaming or shaming yourself (or others), use this as an example to catch yourself so the next time that third evening event comes, you have prior knowledge that your bandwidth is not able to handle it.

By recognizing guideposts and prioritizing guardrails, you leave room for rest, recovery, and recalibration if things go off course. When you fill every moment of your day with activity and events, you become too tired to complete even the easiest of tasks.

FOUR WAYS TO FIGHT DECISION FATIGUE

Another unintentional consequence of going off course is losing your ability to make small, and big, decisions. Decision fatigue hits hard at both work and home. Finding ways to prevent it before it happens, or identify strategies to help stop it, are essential. I've found the following four ways help me when I recognize decision fatigue setting in.

- **Stop**. It sounds like a weird strategy, but when you are overwhelmed and struggling to make any decision, stop making decisions. Taking a break from being in charge, being the boss, or just being the person everyone goes to allows you to breathe and think through things more rationally. In reflection, most decisions I think are "urgent" are rarely even that important. In my mind, I have a perceived time frame, expectation, or ultimatum of getting something done that probably could wait a while to really do well.

- **Drop it.** During the 2021–2022 school year we implemented 88-minute courses, or a block schedule. Knowing the brain development of adolescent learners, we also embarked on a year-long practice of implementing brain breaks during the hour. Teachers had a playlist of activities, and I would visit classrooms, observe brain breaks, and then work with our assistant principal and coaches to provide a feedback loop for all teachers to increase the use of and the variety of brain breaks during the students' day. So, if that practice works for students, why not adults? When you are flustered with making decisions, take a brain break from the activity and turn to complete something else. It could be answering emails, connecting with a teacher, or visiting a classroom. Finding a way to flip activities and try something else might give you the break needed to come back and work on what you started.

- **Walk away.** If you struggle with stopping when you are frustrated, set a timer for 10 minutes and don't think about it. Free up your brain by shifting the focus of tasks. Physical activity, time outside, and time off technology can help shift perspective and bring you back into focus.

- **Try again tomorrow.** This is essential if your guideposts are blowing up and your guardrails are broken. Write down where you left off and sign out of that project for the day. This has been helpful for me, especially during stressful seasons of the year. Learning to pause instead of pushing through has usually ended up with a better product and higher productivity.

GENTLE REMINDER: STOP NEGLECTING THE SIGNS

It is okay to not be okay, but don't use that as an excuse not to find ways to maintain a sense of sanity in stressful seasons. Create a plan to find guardrails during times when everyone seems to be knocking over your guideposts.

Doing the Homework: Guideposts That Your Guardrails Are Gone

List below a few signs of your guideposts:

Looks like _____

Feels like _____

Those around me might notice _____

Guardrails to set up to protect your guideposts:

What guardrails do you need to put up to protect your ability to be a *Principal in Balance*?

CHAPTER 12

Changing Frequencies

It is the time to start aligning the priorities in your life with the time in your day.

#PrincipalinBalance

Overwhelmed? Frustrated? Wondering how in the world you will stick to this new path? And how to course correct all the ways in which you have given all your time to others and have nothing left for yourself? I have seen it called many different things: margin, white space on the calendar, breathing room, etc. Regardless of the buzzword, creating bandwidth in work and life is an essential focus to become a *Principal in Balance*.

Band · width \ 'band-width: the emotional or mental capacity necessary to do or consider something.

So, how do you know when you need to revisit your bandwidth? Often it is too late. You have a blow up at home, you feel burdened at work, or you walk through your day in a blur not really feeling much of anything outside of frustration or fear. Bandwidth is the ability to have space in your day to reflect, renew, and rest.

Reflect: Autopilot isn't a way to lead your life. Breaking the cycle of pushing through the day requires intentional time to pause and utilization of a framework to guide the reflection.

You might consider stacking reflection onto established habits. As part of my morning routine, I say the three things I am grateful for and three things I am looking forward to reflecting on. This not only sets the tone for my day but allows me some quiet time in the morning to reflect on what went well the day before in a structured and intentional manner. Writing it down makes it more meaningful and provides an opportunity to go back to previous years and journals to see how I survived challenging seasons.

Renew: Finding bandwidth is an opportunity to refuel on a regular basis. This doesn't require lavish vacations or days at the spa. Renewal can be a five-minute meditation, a walk outside, yoga or another form of exercise, listening to music, or watching a movie. Honestly, anything that brings you joy is something you need to infuse into a regular routine.

For me, I look at Sundays as my chance to renew and get ready for the next week. This means I am offline most of the time, meaning I don't check email, I do not use my social media accounts as much, and I make time for walks, a movie with the family, or diving into a book that has been sitting on my shelf for a while waiting to be read.

Rest: Yes, rest. Beyond the nap, rest has so many resilient building factors. I can see why our hustle culture hates this. So, what could rest look like? For me, the simplest way to find rest is to let go of everything else.

Rest is essential to ensure not only you are getting bandwidth at home, but you are healthy to return to work the next day. Think about a symptom you have that indicates a lack of rest. For me it is the occurrence of migraines. These sneak up on me, and usually they start in the middle of the night. If I don't catch it in time, the migraine creeps into my workday, diminishing my capabilities to complete the tasks that are normally easy for me. They dampen my ideas and initiatives as I struggle to treat the symptoms while suffering through the workday. Therefore, finding ways to become more preventative might be hard, but it's easier than trying to suffer through reactive symptoms of stress and fatigue.

As an "anti-napper," I have had to work hard to find other ways to seek rest during the week. This has manifested into opportunities to sit and listen.

While we understand what it is, now it is time to find ways to incorporate it into our day.

12-HOUR DAY CHALLENGE

In theory, this sounds easy. In practice, it is much more of a challenge. Plan to separate work and life in a 12-hour time block. This means you can work for 12 hours and then you have to be off for the other 12. In clock math, it could look like this:

12-Hour Challenge	
Work Time	Time Off
7:30 a.m.–7:30 p.m.	7:30 p.m.–7:30 a.m.

Okay, so you might look at this chart and say, "Wait, this is easy!" Well, when you are thinking "time off," you have to include email, phone calls, social media, reading "for work," etc., into that off time.

Oh, yikes. Yes, just because technology is on 24/7 doesn't mean you have to be on it as well. So set up systems in advance to prepare you to complete this challenge. This is where having accountability partners is essential. My two teen boys are more than willing to take mom's phone away when we are watching a TV show as a family. I also have set up "sleep" times on my phone that snooze emails and silence notifications that might keep me from really taking the time off I need.

If you are someone who has notifications on for all work reminders (including email) or feels off when you are not on all the time, consider setting out-of-office reminders on your email. They can be for extended times or just gentle reminders to families and staff of when and how they can reach you. Setting guardrails up to protect your bandwidth is not only okay, it is essential. The next step is finding a margin in your day.

Full is no longer fine. Oh, here we go, that "f" word again. I used to think that the busier I was, the better I was for others. Running from meeting to meeting, committee and commitments with my hair on fire was my standard. I treated busyness like a badge of honor or recognition that I must be good at what I am doing, because I am doing everything. Spoiler alert: epic fail.

When you recognize that less is more and having free time in your day brings back calibration, and guardrails to prevent your guideposts from being blown over, you will live a happier, healthier, and more fulfilled life. And that starts with seeking more margin and a less-booked, less-crowded schedule for the day.

mar · gin \ 'mär-jən : the part of a page or sheet outside the main body of printed or written matter

When I was writing in college, I always wanted to negotiate my own margins. I needed a paper to look longer. I would margin in a way that the page looked fuller. But when I had written too much, and didn't know what to take out, I would go in and make my margins so close to the end of the paper I would worry the words might not all fit on the page and there might be overflow.

Any chance your life feels like this at times? Without margin in our day our minutes overlap, our meetings run over each other, and we don't have time to think, process, or plan from one thing to the next. When you operate without margin, you lose the opportunity to reflect, recalibrate, and refocus on what is to come next. Instead, you operate by the seat of your pants making quick decisions without thinking about long-term consequences.

In work and life, I have operated with limited margin, resulting in inconsistent success. Can I lead this meeting? Sure. Will I do it well and with enough background information? Not as well if I had set aside time on the front end to review the data, check additional resources, connect with other leaders for additional options, and practiced what I wanted to say at least one time.

Leading without margin is like teaching without a sub plan: you have no direction, so you just have to plan on the spot, and hope you are going in the right direction.

If it is so important, how can you find ways to make time for it in your day?

- **Plan ahead.** Taking 30 minutes at the start of your week to plan out your days will help you see where you need to add margin through the week. I review my calendar either on Friday or Saturday for the week ahead. I make note of any meetings I need to have materials/information for in advance, evening activities for school or my boys, and any other special events or activities that are outside the norm. By setting aside this time and reviewing in advance, you can catch tasks that can be put into your batching times in the day or work to schedule time to take on tasks within the workday, so you don't take it home.

- **Build your week.** I am a huge fan of having a foundation to build a weekly schedule. At the start of the year, I map out the big things in my week: building leadership meetings, district meetings, and obligations, and then concerts/games/activities for the upcoming season. After that, I schedule time in my day for the business tasks, such as answering emails, completing paperwork, or calling people back. I also schedule time out of the office and into classrooms. Some of the time I am working directly with students; other times I am using this as a mobile office, one in which I can get work done and stay connected with kids. By creating a template, you can see where you need to adjust margin to build in bandwidth.

- **Batch when you can.** I am a huge fan of batching. This is setting aside time to do similar tasks, and then setting it aside outside of that block of time. Email is a great thing to batch. I set time in the morning when I arrive at work to do my first batch of email, then again around noon and a final time at the end of the day. By batching this task, I am not grazing on it all day or letting it distract me from engaging in a meeting, a classroom, and interaction with others by looking at email as a multitasking activity in the day.

- **Deep work for important projects.** When I have a big project or task, I set aside time and find a distraction-free space to get it done. For me, morning is a better place in the day for my brain to be focused on reading, writing, or researching important work I need to accomplish. If I am working on building the master schedule, I might work from 8 a.m. to 12 p.m. with a few stretch breaks scheduled as needed. But when I am doing the work, I am not doing other things. That means turning off the phone, silencing notifications, and setting alerts in the office that I am not to be disturbed. One summer, Kelly, our building secretary, even put up a sign that said, "Only knock if the building is on fire, otherwise schedule a time with Kelly to talk." That might sound silly or off-putting for those who might need you for just one thing. However, when you set this time aside and schedule in time to talk later, you will have the bandwidth to listen because you won't be thinking of getting the other thing done.

- **Have a system to document the day and calculate your week.** I admit, I can't go many places without my planner. There is something about having it with me as I am trying to navigate my life at work, my family, my passion projects, and upcoming dates. This also helps me reinforce my goals and prioritizes what I have to get done (versus what others are asking me to do). Having it nearby helps me say no to evening events when I already have committed to two nights out that week or saying no to speaking/coaching events when I hit my quota for the month. A planner can be a tool that gives you the guardrails for adjusting your bandwidth during different times of the year.

Finding time to build bandwidth and set margin will give you back time in your day and space in your mind to focus in on your purpose, recalibrate your calling, and be more intentional with time for goal achievement. Be careful of falling into a perfection trap. Remember, if you are pushing against years of busyness and pressure from others to do it all and be everything for everyone, shifting that practice won't be easy . . .

. . . and you won't be perfect at it.

REDEFINING ESSENTIAL AND IMPORTANT: PURPOSE OVER PERFECTION

You may have heard of the Eisenhower Matrix. The point of the chart is to refine and define what is urgent and important. Once you start to filter requests through this type of process, you can better focus in on things you have to do so you can do those things well. This type of framework also helps you pull out and away from things you can delegate, delete, or defer until you have the bandwidth to tackle them.

As you reflect on what needs to get done, and prioritize by urgent and important, add another layer: What can I delegate or delete? Stop playing what we in the Midwest call "Minnesota Nice" and start setting boundaries with email inboxes, requests for your time, and allotment of your resources. As you work to become a *Principal in Balance* it is not only important to use the following steps, but also essential.

- **Don't silo the setbacks.** So, your new dismissal plan flopped, an interaction with a parent didn't go well, or a post on social media went in a direction you hadn't planned. Instead of awfulizing, exaggerating, or internalizing the mistake, find someone to talk to about it. Connecting with other school leaders allows you to see you really are not alone, and chances are they have a story to match or top your failure.

- **Celebrate the successes.** Big or small, it is important to celebrate the wins. Take time every day to reflect on what went well instead of focusing on what went wrong. For me, this gratitude reflection happens during my morning ritual. As I have shared, the daily routine includes writing down three things I am grateful for from the day before and three things I am looking forward to that day. By starting my day with a focus on what is going well, my mindset shifts to stop focusing on what is going wrong.

- **Lean into the compliments more than the criticism.** So often we may focus on the one negative comment that we forget about the five other positive ones that were given. This may seem small, but I keep a good news box under my desk. On the tough days, I open the box and read the notes of encouragement, appreciation, and celebration I have received from staff, families, and students.

- **Turn it off at times.** And one final gentle reminder: principals, turn your title off. Stop checking email at all hours, get the sleep you need, and give yourself grace when things don't go the way you had hoped. While you have been focused on taking care of everyone around you, please make sure you save energy to take care of yourself.

Stop trying to put yourself on a pedestal of perfection. It is okay to realize you are a person just like the rest of us, failures, flaws, and all.

#PrincipalinBalance

As you start to resist the pull of being on all the time and the need to be perfect within this process, you will find a flow in your day and see more margin in the time you have to work, and the effort you put forth in doing it. But how do you navigate this new process when plans are flipped upside down or you come up against a season of stress you didn't intend or have control over?

BANDWIDTH DURING BUSY SEASONS

Finding ways to self-regulate during a stressful season is essential in finishing what you started strong. Preparing to walk into a storm with the necessary bandwidth to walk out as strong as you started requires purpose, pause, and praise in the process.

- **Purpose in planning.** May is exhausting. It is the end of the marathon of the school year and always seems to be sprinkled with extra evening commitments for school as well as spring/summer activities kicking in for my own children. From track meets to spring basketball practices, I seem to be gone more than I am home. This is a perfect example of how I need to be intentional with my time.

  To create more purpose and accountability in my days, each Sunday I complete a weekly preview in my planner. I make sure to outline how many nights I have family commitments, so I really know what I need to say no to, to make sure I get the rest at night and have the bandwidth to be ready for the next day.

- **Pause the pace.** What is that famous line from *Ferris Bueller's Day Off*? "Life moves pretty fast. If you don't stop and look around once in a while, you could miss it." In the race to get grades done, next year's schedules prepared, final newsletters sent, and assemblies organized, it is easy to get caught up in the fast pace to finish the year.

  The danger of pushing instead of pausing is you lose the chance to do your best work. Think about when you are tired, stressed, and frustrated. Was the email you wrote and sent your best? Was the interaction with the student or staff member tougher or terser than needed? Self-regulation means taking the time necessary to be ready for what comes next, and sometimes that requires you to pace down instead of push through.

  During a busy season make sure you have more margin in your day than normal. Leave work at a reasonable hour at least three days a week, and whenever you leave, leave work at work. No email replies at night and try not to send emails out to staff after hours. Modeling boundaries helps give others explicit permission to do the same.

- **Praise in the process.** Too often, we race through the day and we don't give others, or ourselves, the recognition they need. As educators, we can focus on the negative noise and feedback, more than the great things we are doing every day. Flipping the switch and learning how to focus more on the good will pay off in building resiliency for the next few weeks ahead.

By utilizing these steps, you can take control back during a busy season and push against pressures to go too far, too long, or do too much. Navigating a new frequency for bandwidth takes time, practice, patience, and purpose. Living a life with margin is worth the work and will impact the quality of your self-care and soul-care moving forward.

GENTLE REMINDER: GRATITUDE THROUGH THE GRIND

When you are in a stressful season, make sure to find three things in your day you are grateful for and write them down. Take the time to send a text or note of appreciation to someone who is helping you behind the scenes during these seasons. An extra dose of gratitude during a season of grind can help reframe and refocus until you have time to recalibrate.

Doing the Homework: Adjusting the Dial

What type of bandwidth do I need to have the stamina to achieve a better state of balance while working toward achieving the goals I set?

CHAPTER 13

Putting Yourself First

It is an honor to be asked,
it is still okay to say no.

#PrincipalinBalance

"How do you do it all?" is a question I am asked a lot. People seem to mistake doing a few things well for doing it all and doing it well. Like the iceberg visual early in the book, others only see what they can see, not the work underneath the surface that allows me to travel, attend my children's events, and achieve other accomplishments.

Have I written books while holding down a busy full-time position? Yes. Do I travel and work with educators and spend intentional time with my family? Yes. Have I won state and national awards for my work at school, while still finding time for date nights with my spouse? Absolutely.

But in all the yeses above what you don't see are all the times I've said no. I have turned down promotions to stay focused on the work I was doing at home. I have said no to local, state, and national committees that would have looked great on my resume but would have taken me away from home and school. Saying no to attending every event at the school ensures I am at events at the school my children attend. This is a lesson I learned late, but glad I was able to put it in practice when I did.

boundary \ 'baủn-d(ə-)rē: something that indicates or fixes a limit or extent

What I have learned in the work of becoming more balanced is the importance of setting firm boundaries. In Nedra Glover Tawwab's book *Set Boundaries, Find Peace*, she speaks of the different types of boundaries and the many ways we and others violate these boundaries. When it comes to boundaries, she identifies time boundaries as the one we struggle with the most. She goes on to clarify: "Time boundaries consist of how you manage your time, how you allow others to use your time, how you deal with favor requests, and how you structure your free time. People with these issues struggle with work-life balance, self-care, and prioritizing their needs" (2021, p. 75).

Anyone else raising their hand or sinking in their seat right now?

Time is valuable, and as we spoke about in Chapter 9 on self-care, intentional time is necessary to control our lives if we want to lead them well.

So knowing this is important is one thing, but acting on it and prioritizing our boundaries is another thing.

KNOW WHEN TO SAY NO

Setting exciting and achievable goals was something we did early on in this book. When you know what you want, and you are excited about achieving it, saying no to everything else is so much easier. For example, let's say you have a goal to spend more time with your family at night. Having that identified and prioritized will help you say no to the after-school committees, social hours with coworkers and friends, or putting off answering emails until the kids go to bed. When you set a hard stop in your workday, you can ensure you have dedicated time at night to be offline and away from work.

Instead of *doing it all,*
focus on *doing a few* things well.

#PrincipalinBalance

We only have so much time in our days, and we can't spend it all on work and other people. Think about time like your bank account. You don't want to be checking it all the time to make sure you have money deposited. Instead, it is better to say no more and have a large savings than to say yes and feel depleted all the time.

Knowing you need to say no and doing it is the goal. I am a fan of elevator speeches and one-pagers. If I can't verbalize it in a few sentences or write it down in one page (or less), it isn't concise and clear enough to memorize and be able to articulate to others with clarity. Practicing these speeches and declarations makes them easier to implement in the moment.

- *Thanks for the offer, but I already have an evening commitment this week.*
- *Wow, I appreciate the ask, but I will need to say no at this time.*
- *I am working on establishing better boundaries between work and home, so I won't be responding to emails after 5 p.m.*

Another option, especially if technology (and more specifically email) is your boundary kryptonite, is to create out-of-office messages for your email.

I use these all the time when I am on vacation or away from work for a few days. A sample one looks like this:

Greetings,

I am away from the office until Monday. If you need immediate assistance, please contact the school office at XXX-XXX-XXXX. I will respond to these messages when I return.

. . . Ellis Scholars, I will miss you while I am gone and hope you have a great end to the week. Do your best to complete any missing work so you have the weekend to rest, and I will see you next week.

See . . . not so painful, and easy once you have established a few of these to draw from on your day away. But the real trick is not to break your own boundary.

I too often set these out-of-offices, and then "check" email. You know, just in case the building is on fire, I got fired (just kidding), or some other emergency that could only be communicated via email (insert heavy sarcasm). I start to scroll through the emails and respond, after I just communicated I wasn't responding!!!

Scheduling your priorities. It is one thing to say you need more time for yourself. It is a big step to put intentional steps into action to accomplish prioritizing yourself, and putting boundaries around protecting that time.

My morning routine is well protected. Rarely is someone going to call me a 5 a.m. (unless it's an emergency), and with two teens in the house who prefer sleep, I am left alone to accomplish my morning tasks of reading, reflecting, journaling, and exercising.

However, if I need to find margin in my day for self-care or soul-care, I find support to keep that time protected. Putting appointments on your calendar and setting a buffer is essential. Let's say you want to get to your son's soccer game and it starts at 4:15. Set the appointment at 4 p.m. so you are not rushed to leave or make the regrettable choice to just stay at work and you finally look up and it is already late. By putting in that buffer you have more time to shut down from the day and have space to make it to your priorities at home and in life.

Availability over ability. It is hard not to look out the windows and into other people's houses and become envious of appearances. For years,

I would compare my inability to accomplish things to others' abundant availability and seamless joy and ease of the same tasks. I would watch people's posts of parties with families and friends, late evening game nights, or multiple connections at conferences and wonder why I wasn't doing the same things.

A hard lesson to learn and relearn is just because you can, doesn't mean you should.

Just because you *can*,
doesn't mean you *should*.
#PrincipalinBalance

Setting healthy boundaries means you will say no to more than you will say yes.

- No to events or activities that take away from time at home.
- No to committees or coaching your kid's sports because it will spread you way too thin.
- No to happy hours or socials that take you off track from your health goals.
- No to new positions that would be the next right step, but not the right time.

Finding a framework that helps you filter out opportunities is helpful for when you feel like you want to say yes but you know you need to say no. Below are a few prompts to help ground you in the foundation of becoming a *Principal in Balance*.

- What is your purpose and calling in life?
  - *And how are you making time to cultivate it?*
- What fills and refuels you?
  - *And what drains and depletes you?*
- What are your goals in work and life?
  - *And how long will it take to accomplish these goals, and have you allocated time for it?*

- When are you incorporating self- and soul-care into your daily routine?
  - *And what do you have to take off your plate to prioritize it?*
- What are your guideposts and guardrails to keep you on course?
  - Have you set your bandwidth to a realistic frequency you can maintain throughout the year?

What are you working toward? And will this opportunity, event, or activity get you closer to achieving one of these goals you have set? Or will the energy you expend on this put you behind?

Try it out: you have recently been getting up early in the morning to work out. A friend texted you and asked if you wanted to go out for dinner and a late movie, putting you home hours after your new bedtime for your workout.

a. Skip the workout and go out with friends.

b. Say no and stay home.

Is it that easy? Either or seems easy, but saying it aloud right now is really, really hard. So often we say yes, but at our own expense. And while going out with a friend sounds fun, it may pull you away from a long-term goal you are setting. Or, what if you are setting your sights on making more time for friends and families. Setting boundaries and maintaining habits and routines to get the daily tasks done allows you the time for friends and family.

So, you know you need to say no, but how? Asserting yourself and prioritizing yourself takes time, practice, and, most importantly, pause before you respond to any request. When you create the habits and routines to help achieve your goals and stick to them, your calendar can help you say no. For example, when your friend asks you out for dinner and a movie you could respond, "Wow, thanks for the invite, I have an early morning tomorrow, but could we look at Saturday?" The calendar can be your bouncer and buffer for things you know you need to say no to but are afraid to do on your own.

Prioritizing boundaries takes consistent practice. If you waver on responding to requests, there is a higher likelihood you will favor others' needs over your own. Using the calendar is one way to put a boundary up to protect your priorities. Another option is creating an elevator speech. Having a few practiced sentences ready to go can make it easier to say no.

Let's say you are trying to limit caffeine in your diet. When offered something, instead of being polite and perseverating on hurting someone else's feelings, try a patent response such as:

- Thanks for the offer, but I am taking a break from caffeine right now.
- Any chance you have water or tea?
- I am good right now, thanks for the offer.

By practicing in advance, you will have a ready response and have less of a chance of giving in because you already know what you are going to say.

Here is the easiest way to stick with a boundary, but the hardest to do: pause. We always seem to be in a hurry and that constant movement can make us make quick decisions we likely will later regret. By slowing down and waiting longer than you might want before speaking up, you will be more likely to keep the boundaries you set. When a competing priority is knocking at your door, slowing down before you respond gives your brain a chance to catch up to your desires. We often make a quick decision we regret, but we rarely feel bad responding to something we have thought through before saying something.

Counting to five, stepping away, or asking to call someone back are three ways you can put a pause in play before feeling the pressure to respond. When the request comes electronically, you have a little more distance. However, there are instances where you just want to respond to get it done, and you end up adding more to your plate.

QUALITY, NOT QUANTITY

Too often we feel like if we are not on all the time, we are off.

Offline, and not on email 24/7.

Off kilter, unfocused, and frustrated.

Off the charts with worry and anxiety about what we think we should be doing.

Off track on the task list and expectations we think others think we should accomplish.

Here is the new normal: sometimes we have to slow the pace of our current life to get back on track of the life we want to live.

When you are looking for a plateau to pause in the pace of the climb, or to heal from the occasional stumbles backwards (or downward), focus on the quality of what you are doing, not the amount of time it takes you to do it.

I catch myself in the conflict of trying to do it all, all the time, and slowing down (or stopping) to enjoy something for just a minute or two before I continue is important.

For example, do I want to be the mom who gets to every sporting event for their children, but is always multitasking or worrying about what I am not doing while I am there? Or do I want to be the mom who attends the home events and when the kids are at away games I use that time to catch up on work, laundry, or have a date night with my spouse?

At work, do I want to be the one saying yes to every committee, meeting, or knock on the door? Or do I want to be the person who leaves a little margin in their calendar to catch up on tasks so I don't take them home?

Try to stop focusing on how much you think you need to do, and start prioritizing what you want to do well. By doing this, you will find out it isn't how much time you are "on" that matters, but the quality of the time you are on. I prided myself in sharing how little sleep I got the night before and how productive I was during the day. I completely drank the Kool-Aid in regard to the importance of hustle = hard work and being on all the time = being important.

And I paid many prices for those errors in thinking.

When our oldest son was heading into kindergarten, I was starting my dream job: assistant middle school principal. I worked hard to complete the additional licensure for the degree and spent two years in the school already learning the culture and loving the development stages middle schoolers go through in those three critical years. I had read many books, done the research, and was ready to put that knowledge into practice.

The problem was I wanted to be great at all aspects of the job, right out of the gate. My inaccurate equation for this work went like this:

$$\text{Hard work} + \text{Long hours} = \text{Success}$$

- If I stayed in the hallways for every passing time, people would "see" that I was working hard.
- If I grazed on email 24/7 and responded to everything within a 12-hour time frame, people would see how smart and capable I was.

- If I attended most of the after-school events, students would know I cared about them and families would build trusting relationships with me that would have ripple effects in our school community.
- If I joined all the committees and went to all the meetings, people would know I was important and should be at the table.

At first, it started small. I would leave early for work before my husband and son got up. I thought it was just morning breakfast and cartoon time—not a big deal.

Then if I had an evening concert that started at 7:00 p.m., I figured I would just stay after school the three hours between and get work done instead of going home for dinner with the family.

In less than two years, I learned that if I kept going at that pace, I was going to lose my mind, my health, and my family.

It started to leak into the weekends, too. I am not a napper so I figured while Kenny was napping, I could run into work for just a few hours and be back by dinner.

In isolation, these small things didn't seem like such a big deal. However, once they accumulated, I started to really separate from my life and prioritize my work. I lost the purpose of who I was outside of my job. I prioritized the opinions of those I worked with and focused less on the voices closest to me.

This part of my story isn't a part I am proud of, but I think it is important to be honest about how far away from my life purpose I got. So you know that no matter how far away you get, you can always come back.

So how do you move away from the perceived priority of being on all the time, to literally finding time to be bored? Letting go of being the one everyone needs is an ego crusher and attitude adjuster that doesn't feel great in the moment, but you will be grateful later on in the process.

Doing the right work
rarely feels great *in the process,*
but will be worthwhile *in practice.*

#PrincipalinBalance

BOUNDARIES WITH SOCIAL MEDIA

When it comes to social media, it can be an amazing tool for collaboration, innovation, ideas, and support. But when we don't use it in this way, social media can become a trigger for jealousy, frustration, guilt, FOMO (fear of missing out), and a sense of not being enough. When looking through your feed, consider these three questions:

1. **Are you competing or collaborating?** Have you ever felt critical when you see a post of another school having a parade, or a teacher sharing a new tech tool they are using? Instead of criticizing yourself for not doing that, or criticizing them, celebrate! Take the time to post comments, send a private message, or share with others to enhance collaboration and celebration.

2. **Are you grazing or growing?** Do you log in and get lost for hours or are you surfing for specific ideas? Set a timer and put a Post-it near your computer. For example, this week I was really interested in ideas for end-of-the-year material pick-up. I put a timer on, started with specific hashtags I follow, websites for national organizations, and Facebook pages that regularly post on the topic. I gave myself 30 minutes and then when the timer went off, I walked away with some practical tips (and didn't buy anything from those random pop-up ads).

3. **Are you jealous or joyful?** Friend to friend: stop it. Don't worry about someone else's hair, outfits, or how "perfect" they appear. If you are having jealous feelings every time you see a certain person's posts, stop and really think about why. If you have a valid reason (a real-life run-in with that person that has left you feeling hurt or vulnerable), take a time-out and unfollow for a while. If there isn't a reason, reframe. Instead of being jealous, be joyful. Post a comment to cheer them on!

Finding ways to let go of the perceptions, perspectives, and negative comments people post allows you to regain the boundaries to achieve the goals we set at the beginning of this journey. I have often spiraled into thoughts and worries that derailed me from quality time with my family, my work, and my calling.

SERVING OTHERS BY SAYING NO

Boundaries are the biggest hurdle for educators and leaders to set for themselves. We live to help others, serve at all costs, and value ourselves by how much we support others. When you start to say no more often, not everyone will understand.

> "You mean you aren't going to the event this weekend?"
>
> "So, you really can't help tonight? It's just a few hours."
>
> "You are going away, alone? Without your kids or family? Why?"
>
> "I see you posted you had time to read this weekend, but not to come over?"

Sometimes these comments are meant in kindness as a question, but more often they can feel snarky, "aggressive-aggressive," and mean. The people who care about you the most will care enough to give you space to find balance and set boundaries so when you are with them, when you are at an event, and when you say yes to something, you will really be there, be engaged, and be able to do the right work. If you are feeling pressured to do something because of someone else's guilt or shame, give it back.

I have been sucked into the trap of doing something a certain way because I was told to, assumed I had to, or felt pressured by others. When I am interacting and acting as someone else, I never feel happy about how things end up. The project or product is done, but not in a way that is authentically me. I have had to break up with personal and professional relationships that tried to keep me in a corner, attempted to tell me who I was, and, the most painful—tried to tell me how I couldn't lead at work or life.

I have been questioned about my care and commitment to people over positions.

I have been challenged in our family choice to adopt through gut-wrenching comments.

I have been doubted by other leaders by my decision to set boundaries between work and life.

I have been called into question regarding my calling to support all students in finding successful versions of themselves, whatever it takes, and whatever they need.

As I reread these statements, I am reminded that it was painful, hard, and harmful to have those close to me make such hurtful comments. The work that came from walking away from these people was worth it.

Finding ways to let things go isn't easy but always necessary.

#PrincipalinBalance

Saying yes to yourself is worth it. Walk away from those whose comments are not clear and kind, but full of guilt, and possibly envy that you are taking the path less traveled. In my book *Unconventional Leadership,* I write, "If it doesn't challenge you, it won't push you to change your practice" (Cabeen 2020). I urge readers to move outside the box of traditional teaching, learning, and leading to pursue something bigger, greater, and better for our students. Becoming a *Principal in Balance* will push you to take the path less traveled and lead a life worthy of living, regardless of what others are saying about you.

> **GENTLE REMINDER: IT IS OKAY TO NOT GET TO RIGHT, RIGHT AWAY**
>
> I have said it all the way and I will say it in the end: focus on the process, not about getting it perfect. You are going against the grain, challenging the status quo, and, most importantly, sticking up for yourself. Don't quit, you are worth the work.

Doing the Homework: Systems, Flows, and Letting Things Go

When overwhelmed, feeling a loss of control, or starting to sense burnout or blow-ups, use the following framework to guide your feelings and guard your time, mind, and mouth. Finding ways to put boundaries in place to achieve your goals and find better balance takes time, effort, and work that is worth it.

What is going well?	What is not going well?
Why is it working?	*How might you fix it?*

Triple Check:

- Am I calendaring my priorities including self- and soul-care?
- Am I saying no when needed, and limiting the yeses to essential tasks that align with my goals?
- Am I utilizing time daily for grounding, gratitude, and growth?

Conclusion:
A Letter to My Friend

Dear Friend,

It is crazy to think that someday I will be reading this in a book. A goal I set years before a contract, months between rejection letter after rejection letter. While writing this book, I was reminded of the epic fails and incredible celebrations that have occurred by shifting the emphasis of doing it all for everyone to prioritizing myself.

I know you are learning that there will always be something that needs to get done, somebody will always need you, and there will be tugs of guilt when you realize you can't be everything for everyone. You are realizing that to lead well you have to live well, and that means intentionally finding ways to have a life outside of work.

I have three ongoing hopes for you:

1. **That you continue to make time for yourself.** As hard as it is to shut out the noise and static of others and turn off electronics, you have always been glad when you did. You know you always enjoy going offline, off the grid, or away without your cell phone. I hope as you grow, you increase these times and spaces. Creativity, intentionality of time, and opportunity to rest and reset are essential as you grow in your career, your kids get older, and you continue to revise the goals you set for yourself. Carving out space to have fun, enjoy life, and live without your work title will give you the strength and stamina to survive the rough seasons.

2. **That you celebrate your successes.** You are building the muscle to sit in a compliment longer than you focus on a complaint. Reflect on what you are grateful for including (and especially) the work you put forth to accomplish that goal, skill, or to receive an award. Your work

in self- and soul-care will pay off in the capacity you will have to help others and see the good and the growth in every outcome.

3. **That you continue to learn and grow.** There are always new things we can learn and ways we can improve. Keep reading, connecting, and asking questions. Wherever you are, make sure to find plenty of plateaus in the hills and mountains you are climbing. The sustainability of this work requires pauses as you press forward. And while it always seems faster just to push through, you are going to miss the perspectives of others when you don't stop occasionally to sit, rest, and enjoy the view.

I certainly hope you can look back at these years and see more growth than groans, give yourself more grace than complaints, and learn to lean into rest, resets, and recalibrations.

All the best,

Jess

RESOURCES

So, what, now what? How do you lead others as a Principal in Balance?

You got to the end of this work, and you are trying to build resiliency reserves, set goals, create time for self-care, establish soul-care practices, and create bandwidth by setting boundaries. You are enjoying this work, and starting to find more flourish than fine . . . if it is good for you, can it be good for those you serve? And if so, how can you share this work and help others grow? Here are three Gentle Reminders to support those you serve in building their own resilience reserves.

1. Lead by prioritizing people before their positions.
2. Create space for staff to create self- and soul-care plans.
3. Set ground rules for bandwidth and boundaries by modeling and explicitly explaining what and why you are saying no.

Looking for more resources to go deeper in this work? Check out my website for free resources and extension materials at jessicacabeen.com.

Build habits:

Personal	Professional
Habit:	Habit:
Two-Minute Rule to start:	Two-Minute Rule to start:

Positional	Passions
Habit:	Habit:
Two-Minute Rule to start:	Two-Minute Rule to start:

Create your own Morning Routine using the template below.

Principal in Balance Morning Routine

Activity	Time to Complete

Gratitude Template (part of the Miracle Morning)

Three Things I am Grateful for That Happened Yesterday.	Three Things I Am Looking Forward to Today.

Weekly Checklist: a way to track habits and celebrate goal success.

Activity	Day 1	Day 2	Day 3	Day 4	Day 5	Day 6
Journal						
Reading						
Exercise						
Other:						

Gentle Reminder with all these resources: don't forget to take a grace day.

References

Arnold, H. (2018). Emotional leakage. *Psych Central* (22 September). https://psychcentral.com/blog/radical-hope/2018/09/emotional-leakage#1.

Artuch-Garde, R., del Carmen Gonzales-Torres, M., de la Fuente, J., et al. (2017). Relationship between resilience and self-regulation: A study of Spanish youth at risk of social exclusion. *Frontiers in Psychology* 8 (612). https://www.ncbi.nlm.nih.gov/pmc/articles/PMC5397523/.

Brackett, M. (2019). *Permission to Feel: Unlocking the Power of Emotions to Help Our Kids, Ourselves, and Our Society Thrive.* New York: Celadon Books.

Brown, B. (2018). *Dare to Lead: Brave Work. Tough Conversations. Whole Hearts.* New York: Random House.

Buck, C. and Lee, J. (directors). (2013). *Frozen* [Film]. Disney.

Cabeen, J. (2019). *Lead with Grace: Leaning into the Soft Skills of Leadership.* Highland Heights, OH: Times 10 Publications.

Clear, J. (2018). *Atomic Habits: An Easy & Proven Way to Build Good Habits & Break Bad Ones.* New York: Penguin.

Cook, C. (2014). *About the Course | ECFS311x.* edX. https://courses.edx.org/courses/course-v1:UWashingtonX+ECFS311x+2T2015/6f05543c3766417b8f71d08099fbdc70/ (accessed 15 January 2020).

Crowe, C. (director). (1996). *Jerry Maguire.* TriStar Pictures.

Doerr, J. (2018). *Measure What Matters: How Google, Bono, and the Gates Foundation Rock the World with OKRs.* New York: Penguin.

Eichenlaub, M. (2018). The iceberg illusion. SylviaDuckworth.shop (January 3). https://sylviaduckworth.shop/product/the-iceberg-illusion/ (accessed 10 April 2022).

Elrod, H. and Scott, S. (2016). *The Miracle Morning for Writers: How to Build a Writing Ritual That Increases Your Impact and Your Income.* Hal Elrod International, Incorporated.

Flourishing Definition and Meaning. (n.d.). Dictionary.com. https://www.dictionary.com/browse/flourishing (accessed 16 January 2022).

Flourishing Definition and Meaning. (n.d.). Merriam-Webster. https://www .merriam-webster.com/dictionary/flourishing (accessed 16 January 2022).

Goleman, D. (2006). *Emotional Intelligence*. New York: Bantam Books.

Grant, A. (2021). Feeling blah during the Pandemic? It's called languishing. *The New York Times* (3 December). https://www.nytimes.com/2021/04/19/well/ mind/covid-mental-health-languishing.html.

Heath, C. and Heath, D. (2017). *The Power of Moments: Why Certain Experiences Have Extraordinary Impact*. New York: Simon & Schuster.

Hyatt, M. (2018). *Your Best Year Ever: A 5-Step Plan for Achieving Your Most Important Goals*. Mission Audio.

Johnson, S., Cabeen, J., and Johnson, J. (2018). *Balance Like a Pirate: Going Beyond Work-Life Balance to Ignite Passion and Thrive as an Educator*. Dave Burgess Consulting, Incorporated.

Leaf, C. (2015). *Switch on Your Brain: The Key to Peak Happiness, Thinking, and Health*. Grand Rapids, MI: Baker Publishing Group.

Nagoski, E. and Nagoski, A. (2020). *Burnout: The Secret to Unlocking the Stress Cycle*. New York: Random House.

National Institute of Mental Health. (2021). Caring for your mental health (April). https://www.nimh.nih.gov/health/topics/caring-for-your-mental-health (accessed 20 March 2022).

Newport, C. (2016). *Deep Work: Rules for Focused Success in a Distracted World*. New York: Grand Central Publishing.

Parker-Pope, T. (2021). Why self-care isn't selfish. *The New York Times* (6 January). https://www.nytimes.com/2021/01/06/well/live/why-self-care-isnt-selfish.html.

Price, C. (2018). *How to Break Up with Your Phone*. Berkeley, CA: Ten Speed Press.

Saenz, A. (2012). *The Power of a Teacher*. Peoria, AZ: Intermedia Publishing Group.

Sood, A. (2013). *The Mayo Clinic Guide to Stress-Free Living*. New York: Hachette Books.

Tawwab, N. G. (2021). *Set Boundaries, Find Peace: A Guide to Reclaiming Yourself*. New York: Penguin.

Toussaint, A. (2022). 30 minute interval and arms ride. Peloton Cycle Ride. https://members.onepeloton.com/classes/cycling?instructor_id=%5B% 222e57092bee334c8c8dcb9fe16ba5308c%22%5D&class_languages=%5B% 22en-US%22%5D&duration=%5B%221800%22%5D&has_workout=% 5B%22true%22%5D&sort=original_air_time&desc=true&modal=class DetailsModal&clas (accessed 13 January 2022).

Unkrich, L. and Stanton, A. (directors). (2003). *Finding Nemo*. Buena Vista Pictures.

A Wheel of Human Emotions. (n.d.). Phoenix Performance Partners. https://www.thejuntoinstitute.com/emotion-wheels/ (accessed 19 February 2022).

Wu, A. (n.d.). Goals + Success Spectrum. Faster Than 20. https://fasterthan20.com/toolkit/goals-success-spectrum/ (accessed 19 February 2022).

Index

Page numbers followed by *f* refer to figures.